SEEK FIRST HIS KING- DOM

Studies in the
Sermon on the Mount

by Roger Thomas

 ®
STANDARD PUBLISHING

Cincinnati, Ohio

39960

Unless otherwise noted, all Scripture quotations are from the *Holy Bible: New International Version,* ©1973, 1978, 1984 by the International Bible Society. Used by permission of Zondervan Bible Publishers and the International Bible Society.

Sharing the thoughts of his own heart, the author may express views not entirely consistent with those of the publisher.

Library of Congress Cataloging in Publication Data:

Thomas, Roger W.
  Seek first his Kingdom.

  1. Sermon on the mount—Criticism, interpretation, etc.
I. title.
BT380.2.T52   1987   226'.906   87-6438
ISBN 0-87403-210-5

Table of Contents

Preface

I can still remember it as if it were yesterday. I was a youngster at Christian service camp. The leader explained to us that morning that we were in for a special treat. He then introduced a guest who he said was about to share a very important message.

Quietly and with little fanfare, an elderly gentleman walked to the center of the chapel stage. In a calm voice, he began to speak softly. "Blessed are the poor in spirit: for theirs is the kingdom of heaven. Blessed are they that mourn: for they shall be comforted. . . ."

The words were familiar, but still it was a few moments before I recognized what was happening. He was reciting *from memory* the Sermon on the Mount! As a youngster, I was awed with that saintly Christian's grasp of God's Word. But I was also impressed with the content of what he said.

I had, no doubt, heard and read Matthew 5—7 many times before, I had learned the Lord's prayer as a small child in Sunday school and had heard many lessons and sermons on these words of Jesus.

Later, as a teenager, I memorized large sections of the sermon and eventually the entire three chapters. When I began preaching, some of my first sermons came from the Beatitudes. During college, I heard many great sermons and read some of the world's best scholarly works on the Sermon on the Mount. But nothing I have read or heard has had as powerful an impact on my life as did those quiet words I heard nearly thirty years ago.

As I began my study for this project, I couldn't help reliving that day so long ago. It was the combination of simplicity and power that I recalled. That's what still strikes me when I read the Sermon on the Mount. Jesus' words are simple, deceptively simple. But beneath that simplicity lies a power the likes of which the

5

world has seldom seen. It's the power of One who knew what life was all about. But more than that, it's the power of the One who lived the very life He described.

It's that fact more than any other that I have learned as I have continued my pilgrimage through the Sermon on the Mount in the effort that has produced these pages. It's the One who said it, not just what He said, that gives the Sermon on the Mount its power. Those who first heard Him recognized that. They were amazed at His teachings. But more than that, they were amazed at Him and His authority (Matthew 7:28-29).

If that doesn't happen afresh as you read and study the words of Jesus in the pages that follow, all my work and that of the publisher will have been for naught. My prayer is that you will be amazed at Jesus, at His words and teachings, and especially at the extraordinary life He can create in the most ordinary people, even people like you and me.

I must extend special appreciation to my wife and partner in life for her counsel and typing skills and to the One Way Class at Lincoln Christian Church, who first listened to these lessons as we studied the Sermon on the Mount together.

Roger W. Thomas

Introduction

Surveying the Straight and Narrow

One would think that a Scripture passage as popular and well known as the Sermon on the Mount would be easily understood by all. For two thousand years, ever since Jesus first announced these truths to the crowd on the Galillean hillside, His followers have recorded, memorized, and passed on these words. Matthew initiated this love affair with the Sermon on the Mount when he devoted more space to these teachings of Jesus than to any other.

That popularity didn't end with the writer of the first Gospel, either. Historians note that Matthew 5 was quoted more often by the early Christians for the first three centuries than any other chapter of the New Testament, and Matthew 5, 6, and 7 more than any other three consecutive chapters. The literature of the early Christian centuries contains hundreds of sermons, meditations, and commentaries on these teachings.

John Donne later explained the powerful magnetism the Sermon on the Mount has had through the ages when he observed that, "nature hath given us certain elements, and all our bodies are composed of them; and art hath given us a certain alphabet of letters, and all words are composed of them; so, our blessed Savior in these three chapters of this Gospel hath given us a sermon of texts, of which, all our sermons may be composed. All the articles of our religion, all the canons of our church, all the injunctions of our princes, all the homilies of our fathers, all the body of divinity, is in these chapters, in this one Sermon on the Mount" (Vol. 4, Sermon CXXXVI).

Detours on the Straight and Narrow

The popularity of the Sermon on the Mount is, perhaps, exceeded only by the controversy and differences of opinion that have surrounded it. Through the centuries, literally dozens of different schools of thought have developed, each proposing a new way of understanding Jesus. Some of these have proved helpful. Others are nothing less than what some have called "versions and evasions" of the Sermon.

While it is not necessary for the scope of this study to outline all of the different approaches that have been proposed, it will prove helpful to note a few of the dangers that may sidetrack and keep us from clearly hearing what Jesus says.

The first danger is the "Smorgasbord approach." Some read the Sermon on the Mount as if it were a giant ethical cafeteria. "I will take a helping of 'poor in spirit' and an extra portion of the 'Lord's Prayer,' but I'll pass on the 'pure in heart' and on the 'not laying up treasures.'" To do the Sermon on the Mount justice, we must take or leave it as a whole. Picking and choosing the parts that we like the best or are most comfortable with will never do.

A second detour is the "double standard." Here, the tougher parts of Jesus' demands are applied to a special class of believers, but not to the average disciples. The Medieval church developed an ingenious system of interpretation around this approach. The teachings of Jesus were divided into "precepts" and "counsels." The precepts required obedience of all Christians. However, one could choose whether to observe the counsels or not. These tougher demands led to a greater reward and a life of true sainthood, but were otherwise optional. One need not think twice about where the statements concerning turning the other cheek and loving one's enemy were placed.

Another detour, quite common among some of the prominent Protestant Reformers, took another turn but resulted in a very similar effect. Luther and others, while rejecting the concept of precepts and counsels, insisted that not all of the Sermon on the Mount was to be observed by all disciples all of the time. Specifically, Luther divided the believer's life into two different realms of conduct—the private and the public. A Christian might be obligated to "turn the other cheek" in his private life, but as a public official, he was freed from the limiting and dangerous effects of such political conduct.

Others have suggested that the Sermon on the Mount was intended for the day and age in which Jesus gave it and there only. It doesn't apply to believers in the modern world, they say. Jesus, on the other hand, left the definite impression that His teachings were for all who would follow Him. He told His disciples to take

His message and teachings to the far corners of the world. They were to teach new disciples "to obey everything I have commanded you" (Matthew 28:18-20).

Another quite popular detour is to read the Sermon on the Mount as an impossible ideal. "No one can live the kind of life outlined here," it is argued. Jesus' purpose, it is suggested, was to convict us of our utter sinfulness and cause us to cry out for the grace of God. Admittedly, the Sermon does convict us of our disobedience. But it is another matter to insist that Jesus only intended that His words make us feel guilty and not lead us to obedience.

Jesus seems to make it very clear that the wise man is the one who puts into practice what He taught. The fool hears them, but never does them (Matthew 7:24-27). Whatever guilt and conviction result from reading the Sermon on the Mount are intended to do one thing—lead us to change our lives and to do what we have read.

Life: Jesus' Style

It should be obvious already that I want to propose a different approach to the Sermon on the Mount than those outlined in these detours. I contend that Jesus' words were intended for all His disciples, even those in the twentieth century. Moreover, His precepts were given to be obeyed and lived, not just studied and discussed. What Jesus offered was not just another philosophical system or ethical code, but an extraordinary way of life. I am not suggesting that such a life is easy or even that many of us ever successfully attain it. But I do insist that Jesus never intended us to be satisfied with anything less.

The approach to the Sermon on the Mount that follows makes some fundamental assumptions that are best outlined at this point:

First, these three chapters of Matthew's Gospel are the words of Jesus. Matthew certainly summarized what must have been a much longer discourse, but he did so faithfully, under the supervision of the Holy Spirit. The result is a record that contains what Jesus taught.

Second, this was not the only occasion that Jesus taught these truths. He no doubt taught the same lessons over and over again as He traveled from one village to another. At other times, His disciples would ask questions that called for some review and clarification. Nothing in the New Testament or common sense requires a student of the Gospels to conclude that Jesus uttered these words only once at one place to one group of people. This simple observation eliminates most, if not all, of the problems that some Biblical scholars like to cite when comparing Matthew's Sermon on the Mount and Luke's Sermon on the Plain (Luke 6:17-49). Little attention will be given to the differences and similarities between Matthew's and Luke's record. We will simply assume their consistency.

Third, what Jesus taught in these three chapters was also consistent with what He taught throughout His ministry. In fact, the Sermon on the Mount can best be understood in the context of Jesus' total mission.

The Rule of God

According to the Bible, Jesus had one main message: "Repent, for the kingdom of heaven is near" (Matthew 4:17). Matthew further tells us that Jesus "went throughout Galilee, teaching in their synagogues, preaching the good news of the kingdom" (Matthew 4:23; cf. 9:35). Over fifty times, Matthew uses the phrase "the kingdom of Heaven" (or "kingdom of God" as non-Jews were more likely to refer to it) to describe the ministry and teachings of Jesus.

What Jesus meant by this phrase is important in understanding His teachings. When Jesus spoke of the kingdom of Heaven, He wasn't speaking of a political dominion. This was what many in His day expected. The Jews, downtrodden and humiliated by centuries of enemy occupation, yearned for the day when the throne of David would be established again. The Messiah, the one the prophets foretold, would be the one to bring this to pass, so they hoped and prayed. Jesus insisted, however, that His kingdom was not of this world, at least not in the sense that the politicians of His day understood (John 18:33-37). Nor was His kingdom just something that existed in a far off Heavenly realm. While it wasn't a political rule or territory, it was a real kingdom in the real physical world. This was no easier for those who heard Jesus face-to-face to understand than it is for us today. In fact, Jesus termed His teachings "the secrets of the kingdom of heaven" (Matthew 13:11). Even His disciples struggled with His words.

Perhaps the best way to understand what Jesus meant is to think of a kingdom within the kingdoms. The kingdom of God is not a territory or a political regime, but the rule or reign of God in the lives of men and women who submit to Him. When Jesus entered history, He came to demonstrate this rule of God in a way that had never before taken place. He was the King of kings and Lord of lords *in history.* His miracles, His powerful teachings, His victory over Satan on the cross and, finally, in the resurrection were living evidence that the kingdom of God had invaded the kingdoms of men.

Jesus' message, therefore, was to call men to turn (repent) and become a part of that kingdom. They were to turn the control of their lives over to the King of Heaven. No longer was their allegiance to belong to any earthly ruler or nation. Jesus startled His listeners by insisting that entrance into this kingdom required a righteousness that went far beyond even the most religious (Matthew 5:20). His disciples' main concern must be this kingdom. "Seek first his kingdom and his righteousness" (Matthew 6:33). They were to pray "your kingdom come, your will be done on earth as it is in heaven" (Matthew 6:10). The kingdom always comes first.

In the Sermon on the Mount, Jesus set forth for His disciples the radical demands that being a part of that kingdom places on the lives of those who wish to be a part of it. Submission to the will of God, His reign in the life of a disciple, creates dramatic changes. It changes priorities, conduct, and relationships. It begins inside a person, but it doesn't stop there. It affects everything he does and touches.

If it is the *rule of God,* it must be absolute. Nothing must be left outside of His control.

The Problem of God's Will

One final issue needs to be restated before we turn our attention to the context of the Sermon on the Mount. Jesus concluded Matthew 7 with a call to action. The wise disciple, He insisted, is the one who does, not just hears (Matthew 7:24-27). These words were meant to be lived!

For many well-intentioned followers of Jesus, knowing God's will is the central problem of their lives. I have talked with countless Christians, young, and old, who wrestle with all sorts of important issues. Where does God want me to live? Should I take this job or that one? Should I marry? Whom should I marry? On and on the issues go.

After studying the Sermon on the Mount and rethinking the demands Jesus himself placed on those who would follow Him, I am convinced that as important as it is, *knowing* God's will is not really our problem. Our problem is *doing!*

Mark Twain was right when he observed, "It's not the parts of the Bible that I don't understand that trouble me the most. It's the parts that I do understand." Here lies our real problem with God's will. We think that if only we knew for sure what God wanted, we would have no difficulty bringing our lives into line. For most of us, however, the problem is much deeper than that.

If the truth were known, many of us want to know God's will so that we can then decide whether we want to do it. The Lord, however, calls for us to decide, once and for all, that we truly want to do His will. Then and only then does He begin to make His will known. As Don Hillis notes, "A knowledge of the will of God is relative to one's desire to do the will of God. God does not reveal his will to those who are not gladly committed to it."

E. C. Baird put it this way:

> "You ask: What is the will of God?
> Well, here's the answer true;
> The nearest thing, that should be done,
> That he can do—through you!"

How does all of this relate to the Sermon on the Mount? In every way! In fact, if we fail to understand that the main issue of Jesus' message is submission to the will of God, to His rule, we will constantly be caught up in debates over the details of the sermon and miss the main point. We will be stopped at our knowing problem and never get to the doing. This is exactly what Jesus warned against.

No Easy Road

Our first question when reading the Sermon on the Mount must never be, "Will it be easy to live like that?" Rather, we should ask, "What does Jesus ask His followers to do?" That second question forces us to decide that we want to do it, easy or not. Ultimately, this is the question that all of us must face. It is not, "What is God's will?" It is, "Am I willing to submit to God's will no matter what, even before I know it?"

The life Jesus calls for in the Sermon on the Mount is extraordinary in every way. There's nothing easy, simple, or commonplace about it. Yet He calls for even His most ordinary disciples to live that way. That's what makes them salt and light.

Does He demand too much?

Can an ordinary Christian actually live the life described in the Sermon on the Mount?

Humanly speaking, no! On our own, it's hopeless. But that's exactly where the good news comes in. Jesus never asked anyone to live this extraordinary life on his own. Behind every challenge and demand in the Sermon on the Mount lies the promise with which the first Gospel concludes, "Surely I am with you always, to the very end of the age" (Matthew 28:20).

Chapter One

The Two Kingdoms
Matthew 5:1-12

The Beatitudes (Matthew 5:1-12) are perhaps the most misunderstood Scriptures in the entire Bible. This should come as no surprise. They are also the best-known words of the most misunderstood person in history.

To understand these words, one must first understand who Jesus was and what He came to do. He was more than a mild-mannered moral philosopher. The Sermon on the Mount is more than the sweet platitudes that some readers make it out to be.

The Revolutionary Jesus

Jesus did not come to start a religious reformation. His aim was to ignite a revolution. He didn't propose a slight mid-course correction in the path of human events. He called for a totally new orientation, a journey down a road that led in a completely different direction from any mankind had ever traveled before.

He didn't preach ethics or morality. He didn't even propose a "religion" as most people then or even now understood or understand religion. Instead, He announced the kingdom of God—the total, unlimited, uncompromising rule of God in the lives of men. More than that, He claimed to be the only representative of that kingdom on earth. All authority was His (Matthew 28:18).

Once Jesus' life is seen in this light, His death begins to make more sense—*from a human perspective.* His opponents understood Him better than many of His modern disciples. Why would anyone want to crucify the nice, loving, non-threatening Jesus many modern Christians talk about?

As His Enemies Saw Him

Herod saw Him as rival for His throne. The masses hailed Him as a long-looked-for political deliverer. The religious leaders labeled Him demon-possessed. He was a blasphemer, they said. He dared to make himself equal with God.

Neither Herod, the crowds, or the Jewish leaders fully understood the claims of Jesus. But they had this much right; He was anything but non-threatening!

To truly understand Jesus' mission is to recognize Him as a threat to everything for which this world stands. As Jesus put it:

> Do not suppose that I have come to bring peace to the earth. I did not come to bring peace, but a sword. For I have come to turn
> "a man against his father,
> a daughter against her mother,
> a daughter-in-law against her mother-in-law—
> a man's enemies will be the members of his own household"
> (Matthew 10:34-36).

His teachings and ministry could not be forced into the old categories and institutions of the day. New wine required new wineskins (Matthew 9:17).

The King Has Come

Jesus knew exactly what He was doing. He understood that He was an intruder. He was a rival king in another's kingdom.

Satan recognized this as well. The deceiver confronted the Challenger at the very beginning. All Jesus had to do was bow His knee to Satan and all "the kingdoms of the world" would be His. Jesus never questioned Satan's ability to deliver on his promise (Matthew 4:4-10). Jesus refused. To worship Satan rather than God was to abandon His very purpose for coming to earth.

Jesus came to announce the kingdom of God and to call men and women to come voluntarily under its rule. To become a disciple of Jesus meant to decide to which kingdom one was willing to give allegiance. It was either/or! No one could serve both kingdoms. Friendship with one meant war with the other.

The Boundaries of the Kingdom

The Beatitudes outline the differences between these two competing kingdoms. Jesus draws the boundaries that separate the two realms. In what are often wrongly viewed as reassuring words of comfort to struggling humanity, Jesus actually offers a checklist for determining in which kingdom a person is living.

Rather than nice words of comfort, Jesus offers what William Barclay calls "a series of bombshells." He turns normal human values, even common religious values, inside out. At the very least, Jesus proposes a totally different way of approaching life. He offers new priorities, new principles, new dreams, and—most of all—a new king!

Be-Attitudes: the Foundation of Life

A closer reading of the opening verses of the Sermon on the Mount uncovers several important observations. First, Jesus offers a total of nine different blessing statements. The last two (Matthew 5:10-12), which present basically the same truth, form a single unit.

In each Beatitude, the same formula is repeated: "Blessed are the . . . [a quality or characteristic is cited] because they . . . [a reward or promise is indicated]." Each statement is in the third person, "they," except the last blessing, which is repeated in the second person, "you." This change provides a bridge to the paragraph that follows.

The reward or promise for the first and eighth Beatitude is the same: "theirs is the kingdom of heaven." Quite likely, this phrase forms an umbrella that encircles the other six rewards. Jesus doesn't describe eight different people who will receive eight different rewards, but one person—the man or woman who submits to the rule of God. Such a person manifests all of the qualities and receives all of the benefits of the Beatitudes.

The eight statements divide into two sets of four. The first set describes inner qualities (poor in spirit, mourning, meekness, and hunger for righteousness) while the second refers primarily to relationships between people (mercy, peacemakers, purity of heart, and courage in the face of persecution). All eight emphasize character that produces conduct. Myron Augsburger terms these the "be-attitudes." They picture what the disciple is to *be*. From them flows what he *does*.

The last Beatitude brings the entire list into focus. Persecution at first seems like a strange by-product for such peaceful qualities. The world's reaction provides a graphic reminder of how radical and threatening these teachings really are. Such God-like qualities challenge the worst of a godless world. Together these eight "be-attitudes" provide the foundation for the rest of the Sermon on the Mount.

"Blessed": the Key

To appreciate the revolutionary dimensions of the Sermon on the Mount, one must first understand the key word *blessed*. This word is used over fifty-three times in the rest of the New Testament. In Matthew, Jesus describes as blessed those who take no offense at Him (Matthew 11:6) and those who have eyes to see and ears to hear (Matthew 13:16). He calls Peter blessed for his confession of faith (Matthew 16:17) and the faithful servant for awaiting the return of his master (Matthew 24:46, although this is not clear from the NIV translation).

Originally, this term described outward prosperity. The Greeks gave it a religious twist. They used it to describe prosperity that resulted from the favor of the gods. The ancients used the term to describe the Island of Cyprus because of what they considered its near perfect climate and environment.

The Old Testament added an ethical ingredient that was lacking among the Greeks, but the emphasis was still outward prosperity. A blessed man was one who had found favor in the eyes of God and was rewarded with prosperity and success.

English translations of the Bible have rendered the word in various ways. The King James Version used the term *blessed*. Some modern translations have chosen the word *happy*. Both fall short of the radical ring the term must have had for Jesus' hearers. *Blessed* sounds overly religious and removes the discussion from the arena of everyday life. *Happy*, on the other hand, sounds like a psychological condition or a mental attitude. Such modern concepts fail to do justice to what Jesus taught.

Another English term, although perhaps not the best translation, does come closer to preserving the radical nature of the eight "be-attitudes." Jesus wasn't proposing simply a new route to religious blessings or inner happiness. He offered an entirely new definition of *success*. He took a word that suggested material and spiritual success and poured into it completely new content.

Success: the World's Way

One doesn't have to look very far to discover how the kingdom of the world defines success. While I was studying this section of the Sermon on the Mount, I became curious about how our world defines this concept. I knew the plastic images portrayed on the TV and in magazines, but I wanted to look a little deeper. I spent a few hours in our local public library surveying a few of the many contemporary "success" books. *Live for Success, Dress for Success, Eat for Success,* and several others all promised immediate happiness and prosperity for those who were willing to follow a few simple principles.

The steps to success were all variations on the same theme. "Pull your own strings!" and "Look out for number one!" were the most frequent battle cries.

Max Gunther provided the clearest example of the modern success formulas *(Family Circle,* October, 1977). He outlined five no-fail ways to achieve personal success. For Gunther, success equaled wealth. His recipe included the love of money, self-reliance, risk-taking, skepticism of others, and an unrelenting sense of superiority.

Even the modern church often follows the same path. One need only read the most popular Christian books or listen to any one of a dozen different "tele-evangelists" describe the successful Christian. Health, wealth, and power are the sought-after "blessings" of the twentieth century. Christians have so absorbed the values of the world that many see no problem with such teachings.

The kingdom Jesus announced was different! Compare what Jesus offered His disciples with the success promoted by the kingdom of the world:

Blessed are the poor in spirit. The world says the successful are the independent and the self-sufficient. "God helps those who help themselves," we are told. Confidence—even arrogance—marks those who refuse to be victims. The assertive get ahead.

Jesus says that success belongs to the poor and the humble, those who have needs and know it. The kingdom of Heaven includes only those who let God pull their strings because they know they can't pull their own.

Blessed are those who mourn. The world says that the detached and calloused are the real success stories. Those who make it don't have time for sentimentality. Only the weak look back. Nice guys finish last.

Jesus says that sensitivity and brokenness bring success. His disciples know how to weep with others because they have first learned to weep at their own shortcomings. They care because they can still feel their own hurts.

Blessed are the meek. The world rewards those who are willing to do anything to get what they want. "If it feels good, do it" may no longer be the public rallying cry of the "now" generation, but its sentiment still rules the world. Restraint and temperance sound strangely old-fashioned.

Jesus says that the self-disciplined and self-controlled will rule the earth. The others will remain slaves of their own passions. Solomon echoed the same truth, "Better a patient man than a warrior, a man who controls his temper than one who takes a city" (Proverbs 16:32).

Blessed are those who hunger and thirst after righteousness. The world cautions against becoming a moral "fanatic." The sophisticated person must compromise and accept the lesser of evils. Learning to accept one's own fallibility is the highest virtue.

Jesus challenged His disciples to settle for nothing short of moral excellence. He likened their quest for righteousness to the hunger of a starving man for food. He turned ambition upside-down and aimed it at righteousness instead of riches.

Blessed are the merciful. The world's citizen is hard-nosed and strict. The weak-willed always lose. Only those who cultivate the killer instinct win. Jesus' people are compassionate and forgiving. They can do no less because they have tasted the grace of God.

Blessed are the pure in heart. The world applauds the urbane, the sophisticated man or woman of the world. Jesus commends the pure, those with a single-minded devotion to what is right.

Blessed are the peacemakers. Competitiveness is the key to the world's game. Fighting, scratching, clawing one's way is the only way to the top. In Jesus' family, peace is the rule. Peacemaking is the name of the game.

Blessed are the persecuted. Popularity is success in the kingdom of the world. Becoming unfashionable is the worst of fates. The wise read the polls and adjust their standards accordingly. The citizens of Heaven's kingdom display courage against all odds. They are willing to take a stand even if it means standing alone. Adversity and opposition are welcomed because God's men have always found it better to be right than to be popular.

In these "bombshells," Jesus sets forth a kingdom like no other on earth. What He outlines makes no sense to many who have decided to walk the broad way and enter through the wide gate. But for those who are willing to listen long enough to hear the promises and the Promiser, the destination makes the journey well worth the demands.

A would-be disciple must be careful however. These "be-attitudes" are not offered *cafeteria-style.* One can't pick his favorites and leave the rest. No one can decide to take a helping of peace-making and mercy, but pass on the poor in spirit and the hungering and thirsting for righteousness. They all are a part of the package. The disciple makes the choice to travel this path when he decides to join himself to King Jesus! Nor are these qualities the possession of a few special saints. What Jesus described may be rare in the kingdom of the world. In His kingdom, they are the extraordinary marks of the ordinary Christian.

The Beastly Alternative

One hundred years ago, C. S. Blackwell offered another fitting description of these beatitudes. In the *Christian Standard* (August 6, 1887), he wrote:

> The antitheses of the beatitudes are the marks of savage communities. They belong to the animal side of our nature. A bulldog can be courageous, but is he likely to be "poor in spirit"? A cock can crow, but can he "hunger and thirst after righteousness"? A peacock can strut, but would you take him as a model of "meekness"? A tiger can fight, but does he occur to you as a type of the "peace-maker"? No, the possession and practice of the beatitudes distinguish the man from the brute. They are the very essence and pith of genuine manhood. It is the fashion in these days to talk about "muscular Christianity." I will tell you what requires Christian muscle—it is living up to the beatitudes. They are really the dynamic forces of time.
>
> The lightning that blasts is salvoed by thunder; but the sunlight that heals and gives life is noiseless as silence. The conquering forces in Christ's kingdom for all time are precisely these beatific graces. The crowned Conqueror of the eternities—who is he but the meek, merciful peace-making, persecuted Lamb of God?

The Perfect Example

Jesus had a right to outline such a radically different kingdom. He lived it every day of His life. He practiced what He preached.

Napoleon, the greatest general and empire builder of his day, said of Jesus, "Alexander, Caesar, Charlemagne, and myself, we all founded great empires. But upon what did the creations of our genius depend? Upon force! Jesus alone founded His empire upon love. To this day, millions would die for him."

Behold! Your king!

Chapter Two

The People Who Change the World
Matthew 5:13-16

Colonel Heath Bottomly, veteran Air Force pilot and war hero, tells of a fascinating experience from his childhood in his book *Prodigal Father.* His dad had taken Heath and his six brothers on a hike into the mountains of Glacier Park in Montana.

On the edge of a giant glacier, the elder Bottomly showed his sons a small icy stream that tumbled over the side of the mountain to the valley below. At precisely that point, the little stream reached the Continental Divide. Part of the stream split and fell to the West, while the other half eventually flowed down the east side of the mountain making its way toward the Atlantic Ocean.

The boys watched spellbound as their father explained the wonder of what they were seeing.

As they were heading back down the trail, young Heath sneaked away from the group and made his way back to the stream. When his father came to retrieve his nine-year-old son, he was lying on the ground at the edge of the precipice with a hand in the middle of the tiny, icy waterfall. As his dad moved his fingers, Heath turned the direction of the flow, first one way and then another.

After removing his boy a safe distance from the edge of the cliff, Heath's father looked him square in the face and said, "Son, I'm proud of you. You're nine years old and already you are trying to change the world! I watched you. That water was going into the Atlantic Ocean and you deliberately pushed it into the Pacific!"

"My soul was afire," Bottomly later wrote. Thoughts of the amazing power of man raced through his head. "With one hand I can change the face of the earth. From now on the Atlantic will be a little shallower and the Pacific a little deeper!"

he world has always been the task of Jesus' people.
Christian, equipped with the authority and power of
: ability to change history forever. He can do far
...more than raise or lower the level of oceans. The Christian can
rescue others from the grasp of Satan's kingdom and introduce
them to the reign of Jesus. He can reach out and touch the hurts
and needs of suffering people, demonstrating the transforming
love of God.

The faith-filled, Spirit-led Christian can turn the world right-
side up.

This was Jesus' message to that fledgling church of misfits and
social outcasts that He called to be His disciples. They were small
in number and had few resources as far as the world about them
was concerned, but they had a giant-sized mission. Jesus didn't
commission them to start a new religion or to reform an old one.
They were to change the world!

How could their task be any less? They were ambassadors of
the kingdom of Heaven!

Go Make Disciples!

Jesus reminded his disciples of their world-changing ministry
many times. He first sent the Twelve, equipped with Jesus-power
to heal the sick and to cast out demons among their fellow Jews.
"As you go," He told them, "preach this message: 'The kingdom
of heaven is near'" (Matthew 10:7).

Later, He sent out seventy-two followers with the same task.
"The harvest is plentiful, but the workers are few. Ask the Lord
of the harvest, therefore, to send out workers into his harvest
field. Go! I am sending you out like lambs among wolves," He
warned them (Luke 10:2, 3).

After the resurrection, Jesus widened the scope of their mission. No longer were they just to call their fellow Jews to follow
King Jesus. The whole world, Jew and Gentile, was their mission
field. Matthew concludes his book with these new marching
orders. "All authority in heaven and on earth has been given to
me. Therefore go and make disciples of all nations, baptizing
them in the name of the Father and of the Son and of the Holy
Spirit, and teaching them to obey everything I have commanded
you. And surely I am with you always, to the very end of the age"
(Matthew 28:18-20).

The first announcement of this world-changing ministry came at the very beginning of Jesus' ministry. "Come, follow me ... and I will make you fishers of men," He told those first two fishermen-turned-evangelists (Matthew 4:19). Little did they know the full extent to which those few little words would change their lives.

The Charter of His Kingdom

Most of the Sermon on the Mount is directed at the private life of the disciple. Jesus stressed attitudes, personal morality, and private activities like prayer and fasting. Yet, even here, He carefully reminded His followers that they were not just to be good, privately pious and proper. They were to be good for something! They were to be salt and light *in the world!*

To understand this statement fully, it is important to remember how it fits into the structure of the Sermon on the Mount. Jesus began by outlining seven marks of the disciples' character, the inner attitudes and dispositions that set them apart from the world (Matthew 5:3-9). The eighth Beatitude and the elaboration that followed it formed a transition. Jesus systematically turned the focus away from the disciple's own inner character and toward the world's response.

The eighth Beatitude should have removed any doubt about the revolutionary nature of His Kingdom. The first seven Beatitudes were more than pious platitudes about keeping a positive mental attitude in the face of adversity. Whatever their understanding of His words, the disciples knew one thing for sure; they weren't going to win any popularity contests for being pure and meek. He warned them to expect opposition, even open persecution.

Christ-like character flows from allegiance to a different king. Since kings can be very jealous of their rivals, the "prince of this world" doesn't take too kindly to those who "hunger and thirst for righteousness." The righteousness of God's kingdom is a threat to the kingdom of this world! It always has been and it always will be!

How to Beat the Devil

When confronted with persecution for righteousness, the follower of Jesus has three immediate choices. He can either fight, he can flee, or he can fold. He can return "fire for fire" by fighting the devil on his terms. He can seek sanctuary somewhere isolated from the world's battles. Or he can give up and abandon the faith. None of these alternatives solves the problem. In the first case, fighting worldliness with more worldliness is self defeating. It is surrender.

Flight is also surrender. To flee the world, or to attempt it, is to hand over the world to evil. Attempted seclusion acknowledges that the kingdom of God is no match for the kingdom of this world, an idea that the adversary has been peddling since Eden.

The third choice is such blatant surrender that it needs no further comment. Jesus directed His disciples to travel another path. His goal was victory over the world. He told them to counteract evil with an even more powerful strategy. Paul understood this tactic well and outlined it in the clearest possible terms:

> Do not repay anyone evil for evil. Be careful to do what is right in the eyes of everybody. If it is possible, as far as it depends on you, live at peace with everyone. Do not take revenge, my friends, but leave room for God's wrath, for it is written, "It is mine to avenge; I will repay," says the Lord. On the contrary:
> "If your enemy is hungry, feed him;
> if he is thirsty, give him something to drink.
> In doing this, you will heap burning coals on his head."
> Do not be overcome by evil, but overcome evil with good (Romans 12:17-21).

The remainder of the Sermon on the Mount describes the overcoming life of the disciple. Jesus first insisted that the kingdom life far exceeds the phony righteousness of even the most respected religious zealots of His day. He then cited example after example of the "salt and light" lived by His disciples. He first spotlighted their personal ethics (Matthew 5:21-49), then their public religious activities (Matthew 6:1-18), their priorities (Matthew 6:19-34), and finally their relationships with others (Matthew 7:1-12). Each exhortation and illustration combined with the others to paint a living portrait of the kingdom-disciple.

Matthew 5:13-17 includes two pronouncements, two parables, and one concluding principle. First, consider together the pronouncements and the parables.

Jesus offered two startling word pictures of His followers. Technically, the phrases He used are metaphors—"you are the salt of the earth"—"you are the light of the world." He didn't tell them what they *ought* to be, He announced what they *already* were if the world-changing qualities of the Beatitudes were present in their lives. Both metaphors communicated very definite ideas to Jesus' first-century listeners.

Salty Saints

The people of Jesus' day considered salt a very precious, and sometimes rare, commodity. It was so necessary a part of everyday life that the Romans placed a heavy tax on it to increase the revenues of the imperial treasury. At one point, the Roman army issued a part of its soldiers' pay in salt. The modern term *salary* most likely came from this practice.

Those who lived in Palestine secured salt from two different sources. Along the Mediterranean, people placed salt water in containers or in holes in the sand. When the sun evaporated the water, a relatively pure salt remained. More commonly, the vast salt deposits near the Dead Sea provided opportunities for both private and commercial mining operations. The resultant product, however, left much to be desired. With the salt came many other compounds that looked like salt but, at best, merely diluted its effectiveness. At worst, the contaminants made the salt totally unfit for human consumption.

A popular story of the time illustrates another problem caused by the contaminated salt. According to the legend, one citizen attempted to evade the Roman salt tax by secretly importing a large quantity of the substance and storing it until he needed or decided to sell it. Unfortunately the storage containers in which he had the salt were not water tight. When the rains came, it soaked into the salt, dissolving and carrying away much of the sodium chloride. When he later opened his salt bins, everything looked fine. They contained the same white crystals he had placed in them. However, when he tried to use it, he found saltless salt.

Salt served a variety of purposes in ancient times. It preserved meat and other foods when refrigeration and other forms of preventing decay didn't exist. It also possessed antiseptic qualities. Hebrew midwives, for example, rubbed newborn infants with salt (Ezekiel 16:4).

Job spoke of the most common use for it when he asked, "Is tasteless food eaten without salt?" (Job 6:6). Used in small quantities, salt served as a form of fertilizer by stimulating the root growth of certain crops while at the same time killing surface weeds. Many organic gardeners still advocate its use on asparagus and other garden crops. In heavy concentrations, the same salt could leave a field permanently sterile. Abimelech's armies sterilized the city of Shechem by scattering salt over the ruins (Judges 9:45).

Two other uses of salt involved customs less familiar to us. For reasons not completely clear to us, the law of Moses commanded certain sacrifices to be salted before they were offered to Jehovah (Leviticus 2:13; Numbers 18:19; Ezekiel 43:24). This may be partly explained by the fact that salt was also an essential part of the ratification of convenants and treaties among many people in the Middle East (2 Chronicles 13:5). To eat salt with another person meant the same thing as we would more likely term "breaking bread." It described fellowship and friendship. Therefore, it became customary for former enemies to eat or at least exchange salt when agreeing to terms of peace. It was only natural then that any peace offering or other sacrifice that portrayed man's approach to God would involve this same custom.

In the New Testament, salt was used as a metaphor for the disciples' commitment (Luke 14:34, 35) and the sacrifice that faithfulness required (Mark 9:49, 50). James used the contrast between salt and fresh water to illustrate the need for pure speech (James 3:12). Paul also referred to the Christian's speech, but called for words "seasoned with salt," which would present a positive witness to unbelievers (Colossians 4:6).

Lighting the Way

For the ancients, turning on the light was a bit more complicated than flipping a switch. Common lamps were very primitive devices by today's standards. Typically, a poor family would simply use a small clay dish with a small wick partially submerged in oil. At best, the lamp provided only a limited amount of light. Sometimes, when a person wanted to darken the lamp without extinguishing the flame, as might be the case when fire was in short supply, a small cover would be placed over the lamp. The bushel or peck measure that Jesus described may have been a clay pot used as a cover.

Light was a common figure of speech among people familiar with the Old Testament. It was symbolic of God's presence. Darkness represented sin and evil (Job 12:25; 24:13; Luke 16:8; John 1:3; 1 John 1:5-7). The Old Testament described the Messiah of

Israel as a light that would shine in darkness (Isaiah 42:6; 49:6; Luke 1:79; 2:32). When Jesus said He was the light of the world, most who heard Him knew exactly what He meant (John 8:12).

The Old Testament also promised that Israel, the people of God, would become a "light to the Gentiles." Nations would come to the light of Zion (Isaiah 60:1-5). "If you spend yourselves on behalf of the hungry and satisfy the needs of the oppressed," the Lord promised, "then your light will rise in the darkness, and your night will become like the noonday" (Isaiah 58:10).

The New Testament picked up this same theme and applied it to the church. "For you were once darkness, but now you are light in the Lord," exhorted Paul.

> Live as children of light (for the fruit of the light consists in all goodness, righteousness and truth) and find out what pleases the Lord. Have nothing to do with the fruitless deeds of darkness, but rather expose them (Ephesians 5:8-11).

Christians who remain faithful are "sons of the light and sons of the day" (1 Thessalonians 5:5).

To what did Jesus refer with His illustrations of the salt and the light? Simply this—His disciples have a purpose in the world. Like salt that preserves against decay or enhances the flavor of something bland, the citizens of the kingdom turn a sometimes stinking, flavorless world into something fit for human habitation. Their light dispells the darkness, exposing sin and calling attention to the righteous reign of God.

To this announcement of purpose, Jesus added a warning. Like savorless salt and hidden light, a disciple that fails to change his world is useless. Good for nothing! Instead, Jesus called the citizens of His kingdom to let their light shine through their good deeds so that men would glorify God.

What Will It Take?

For salt to do its job, two simple conditions must be met, both of which apply to the disciples' witness. First, the salt must be pure. Contaminated or diluted sufficiently, the salt is worthless. Unless a Christian's life demonstrates a holiness and purity that makes it significantly different from the watching world, his witness will lack credibility. His value to the world and to God stands in direct proportion to his uniqueness.

Paul called his readers to "become blameless and pure, children of God without fault in a crooked and depraved generation." Instead, they were "to shine like stars in the universe" (Philippians 2:15, 16). "Do not conform to the evil desires you had when you lived in ignorance," warned Peter. "But just as he who called you is holy, so be holy in all you do; for it is written: 'Be holy, because I am holy'" (1 Peter 1:14-16).

Holiness is no small problem for the contemporary Christian. The late Joe Bayly, Christian publisher and author, put this problem in focus when he noted:

> I don't think any observer would dispute the fact that the evangelical Protestant subculture has been overrun by the general American culture's values. If divorce rates have risen in the general culture, they have also risen among evangelical Protestants. If abortion has been accepted in the general culture, objection to it has weakened in the evangelical subculture. Evangelical Protestants follow a similar pattern of TV viewing, of materialism, and other cultural changes *(Pastoral Renewal,* October, 1984, p. 43).

While Christians may not need to reject every custom and fashion of their world, they must live by different moral and spiritual standards. For the "salty" Christian, moral purity is no option. It's standard equipment!

But even the best salt is useless as long as it stays in the salt shaker. It must come in contact with whatever it is to season. For the Christian, this is the flipside of the call to holiness. He must live in the world but not of the world. If he isolates himself totally and completely from the world, he is no better than a light covered by a bowl.

The young William Penn was once asked by an acquaintance to take him to a Quaker meeting in London. The future founder of Pennsylvania did so.

When he and the friend sat through an hour of silence, the friend asked Penn, in a whisper, "When does the service begin?" Penn's answer was, "The service begins when the meeting ends."

An Extraordinary Testimony

An ancient Christian document, probably from the second century, provides an eloquent testimony of the power of "salty" Christians. Listen to a portion of the letter to Diognetus:

28

Christians are not distinguished from the rest of mankind by either country, speech, or customs; the fact is, they nowhere settle in cities of their own; they use no peculiar language; they cultivate no eccentric mode of life. . . . Yet while they dwell in both Greek and non-Greek cities, as each one's lot was cast, and conform to the customs of the country in dress, food, and mode of life in general, the whole tenor of their living stamps it as worthy of admiration and admittedly extraordinary. They reside in their respective countries, but only as aliens. They take part in everything as citizens and put up with everything as foreigners. Every foreign land is their home, and every home a foreign land.

They marry like all others and beget children; but they do not expose their offspring. Their board they spread for all, but not their bed. They find themselves in the flesh, but do not live according to the flesh. They spend their days on earth, but hold citizenship in heaven. They obey the established laws, but in their private lives they rise above the laws. They love all men, but are persecuted by all. They are unknown, yet are condemned; they are put to death, but it is life that they receive. They are poor, and enrich many; destitute of everything, they abound in everything. They are dishonored, and in their dishonor find their glory. They are calumniated, and are vindicated. They are reviled, and they bless; they are insulted and render honor. Doing good, they are penalized as evildoers; when penalized they rejoice because they are quickened into life. The Jews make war on them as foreigners; the Greeks persecute them; and those who hate them are at a loss to explain their hatred.

In a word; what the soul is in the body, that the Christians are in the world.

The Worst Criticism

In the battle between the kingdom of God and the kingdom of this world, the worst criticism that anyone can level at the church or Christian individuals is that they are good for nothing. The day any church or Christian ceases to be a positive force for righteousness is a day of victory for Satan and his warriors. The only justifiable reason for Christian existence is to glorify God by being good for something.

Chapter Three

The Pursuit of Righteousness
Matthew 5:17-20

If the Sermon on the Mount were a modern sermon or address, Matthew 5:17-20 could rightly be considered the proposition or thesis statement of the discourse. In this one paragraph lies the gist of the entire three chapters. Everything else is an exposition of the principle Jesus sets forth here.

Jesus began by outlining the inner character of His kingdom's subjects (Matthew 5:1-12). He then described the impact the citizens of His kingdom could have upon the watching world (Matthew 5:13-16). He here outlined the differences between the conduct of His disciples and the loyal citizens of the world, even religious citizens. The contrasts He described involve ethics (Matthew 5:21-48), religious practices (Matthew 6:1-18), priorities (Matthew 6:19-34), and interpersonal relationships (Matthew 7:1-12). These differences provide the practical application of the qualities announced in the Beatitudes and, at the same time, reveal the ingredients of the Christians' saltiness.

The Kingdom Is Coming

Imagine the reaction of a faithful Pharisee or other religious leader to the preaching of Jesus. "Repent, for the kingdom of God is near," He announced. "The kingdom of God is *near?*" they thought. "What does He mean? What does He think we have been a part of all our lives? And our fathers before us?"

Their reaction was no different than yours or mine would be if someone stepped into the pulpit of our church some Sunday and proclaimed, "Get ready, I'm going to start a true church in this town!" We wouldn't like what that implied about *our* church. Right or wrong, our defenses would swing into full gear. We would have some questions we wanted answered of the new reformer.

Jesus proceeded to answer the questions that were no doubt being asked by those who heard His preaching. He wanted them to understand clearly the relationship of His new kingdom to what had gone before. He wanted to clarify two potentially dangerous misunderstandings of His mission.

Down With Moses

First, some thought Jesus was claiming to be the leader of a totally new religion. They accused Him of blaspheming the temple and rejecting what Moses had taught and stood for. He may have claimed to be a Jew, but His teachings and religious practices revealed a rejection of everything a true Jew considered important, so some concluded.

To this day, devout Jews find it difficult to believe that a person could convert to Christianity without rejecting all of his Jewish ancestry and tradition. Those who claim to be Hebrew or Messianic Christians explain that for them, it is not an either/or situation. In fact, Christianity is not anti-Jewish. Properly understood, it is the most Jewish-affirming faith in the world.

For Jesus, this accusation had a double edge. Not only was it a distortion of His teachings, but it created an insurmountable barrier to understanding who He really was. Jesus claimed to be the one predicted by the prophets. How could He be the long-awaited Messiah and reject the very faith He came to deliver?

It is easy to be harsh with Jesus' adversaries. In all fairness, we must admit that their conclusions did have some basis in fact. Jesus had a habit of breaking the laws of the Jewish faith that many considered most precious. Nothing was more Jewish than the Sabbath. Jesus not only failed to reprimand His disciples for picking grain on the sacred day, He even healed a lame man and then told him to carry his bed away. On the Sabbath! (See Matthew 12:1-14.)

Neither did Jesus' disciples fast as the more devout Jews did (Matthew 9:14-17). He also rejected the need for the various purification rites held sacred by the Pharisees (Matthew 15:1-20). His teachings even cast doubt on the necessity of the all-important regulations concerning Kosher foods (Mark 7:19).

Needed: New Wineskins

Jesus didn't attempt to hide the differences between His teachings and the regulations considered authoritative by the Jews of

His day. To follow Him while holding on to the traditions of their religion was like putting new wine in old skins, Jesus warned (Matthew 9:16, 17). Sometimes the old and the new don't mix. Those who heard and understood Jesus knew that they had to make a choice. They could either follow Him and make some changes, or they must reject Him. If their kingdom was the kingdom of God, as they believed, then Jesus' kingdom must belong to another power. He must be of the devil, they reasoned (Matthew 12:22-32).

Those who simply observed Jesus from a distance may have come to the opposite, but equally mistaken, conclusion about Him. For many, Jesus was just another rabbi. He taught from the same Scriptures, worshiped in the same synagogues, and observed the same religious festivals as other Jewish teachers. On the surface, only minor differences existed between His kingdom and that proclaimed by so many others.

Those tempted to discount the ministry of Jesus in this way were mistaken. He was different! What He offered was not just a slight reformation of the same old religion. His own claims, the claims of the disciples who knew Him well, and even the testimony of His opponents made it very clear that Jesus could not be dismissed as just another traveling rabbi!

The Oldest Kingdom of All

Contrary to these two mistaken notions about His ministry, Jesus offered a third choice. While His kingdom was opposed to everything for which the self-proclaimed religious authorities of His day stood, it was not opposed to the Old Testament. In fact, He wasn't even announcing a *new* kingdom. He was simply proclaiming the oldest kingdom of all, the kingdom of the God of Abraham, Isaac, and Jacob!

To explain this claim, Jesus set forth two fundamental principles that explained the relationship of His ministry to the Old Testament and the perversions of it that were so common in His day. Both principles rest on the same foundation. His Kingdom, He declared, does not consist of rules or a program for religious reformation, but in a radical relationship with God. Jesus claimed that He alone could make that relationship possible.

First, Jesus insisted the He was the fulfiller of the Old Testament. "I have not come to abolish [the law or the Prophets] but to fulfill them," He said. When Jesus spoke of the Law and the

32

Prophets, He was speaking of the whole of the Old Testament Scriptures. For the Jew, these two terms described their Bible. Later in the Sermon on the Mount, Jesus would say that what we have come to call the "golden rule" summed up the Law and the Prophets (Matthew 7:12). Toward the end of His ministry, He answered the query of His accusers by declaring that "all the Law and the Prophets hang" on the commandments to love God and to love man (Matthew 22:40). The weekly readings of Scripture in the synagogue came from the Law and the Prophets (Acts 13:15). Paul insisted that everything in his faith agreed with the Law and Prophets (Acts 14:14). For whatever reason, in Matthew 5:17, Jesus altered slightly the normal expression. He spoke of the Law *or* the Prophets, rather than the Law *and* the Prophets.

"I Love Thy Law, O Lord!

Throughout His life and ministry, Jesus displayed the highest appreciation and gratitude toward the Old Testament. He obviously knew the Old Testament well. He quoted it when faced with personal temptations (Matthew 4:4-11). He taught from it or referred to it when teaching. Scripture was His final court of appeal on matters of ethical and theological controversy (Matthew 22:29-32, 37-40; John 5:39-47). He believed the historical record of the Old Testament, citing its events and using its people as illustrations of spiritual and moral truths (Matthew 10:15; 11:23, 24; 24:37-39; Luke 11:51; John 8:36). Even when not directly reading or quoting the Old Testament, Jesus saturated His teachings with expressions and allusions that came straight from the Law and the Prophets. Most importantly, the Old Testament was His primary source for explaining His own life and mission (Luke 4:21; 24:25-47).

Jesus would have had nothing to do with attempts, ancient or modern, to drive a wedge between faith in Him and confidence in the authority of the Old Testament. He taught His first-century disciples to believe and respect it. His twentieth-century followers dare not be satisfied with anything less.

The Completer Has Come

Jesus explained His relationship to the Law and the Prophets in negative and positive terms. First, He did not come to *"abolish"* them. The term He used was a powerful one. It described the physical act of tearing down a house or the legal process of annulling or setting aside a law. He was neither a law breaker in His personal life or a law destroyer in His ministry.

Instead, He came to *"fulfill"* the Old Testament. This expression was used in many different contexts. It referred to making something full in a physical or literal sense. It also described the act of completing a period of time. It was the common term used to explain a prophetic event that finally came to pass.

Exactly how did Jesus fulfill the Law and the Prophets? Ever since the writing of the New Testament, Bible scholars have wrestled with this question. Augustine, for example, listed six different answers. He claimed that Jesus fulfilled the Old Testament first by obeying its commands. Second, through the Holy Spirit, He made it possible for His followers to obey it. He also expounded its true meaning in His teachings. Next, He brought to pass in His life and deeds the predictions that were promised by the prophets. Fifth, He transformed the ceremonial regulations and rituals of the Old Testament by giving them a deeper meaning and eternal purpose. Finally, Augustine taught that Jesus fulfilled the law by offering new teachings that furthered the intention of the old law.

Jesus wanted His disciples to understand that a new day was dawning. God was in the process of dropping the curtain on the final act of the Old Testament drama. Soon He would tell the crowds who followed Him that "all the Prophets and the Law prophesied until John" (Matthew 11:13). Something new was about to happen that would radically change the world's understanding of everything in the Old Testament. "This is what I told you while I was still with you," He reminded His disciples later. "Everything must be fulfilled that is written about me in the Law of Moses, the Prophets and the Psalms" (Luke 24:44).

Paul, who probably understood the Old Testament better than anyone else in the early church, said that God's purpose for the law was to lead men to Christ. He described the Old Testament as a "schoolmaster" (Galatians 3:24, KJV) whose purpose was to prepare his students for something yet to come. The Greeks used the term to describe a slave who cared for the young children of the family until they grew old enough for a more formal education. Someday, the schoolmaster's task would be completed.

Jesus fulfilled the Law and the Prophets not just by being the one they predicted but by also being the very reason for which they existed. Matthew emphasized this repeatedly in his Gospel.

Over a dozen times in his account of Jesus' life and ministry, he noted events from the Old Testament that Jesus "fulfilled" (cf. Matthew 1:22; 2:15, 17, 23; 4:14; 8:17; 12:17; 13:35; 21:4; 26:54, 56). These included predictions, but they also included something else. Time and time again, Matthew pointed to non-predictive statements in the Old Testament as evidence of Jesus' messiahship. For example, in its Old Testament context, Hosea 11:1 had nothing to do with the return of the young Jesus from Egypt. But Matthew made a connection between the two (Matthew 2:15). His purpose was to show that Jesus also fulfilled a pattern that had permeated all of God's dealings with man since creation. Only in Jesus, Matthew insisted, could God's relationship with man be understood. *Everything* God had done since Eden was in preparation for Him.

Many today read Jesus' words and miss the main point. He did not say that the law would never disappear. He said that though heaven and earth should disappear, not the slightest stroke would disappear from the law *"until everything is accomplished."* In Jesus, it was all accomplished to the smallest detail.

The Law Today

What, then, is the status of the Law and the Prophets today? The same as it has been for almost two thousand years! The Old Testament stands fulfilled! Its purpose was to prepare the way for Jesus. He came and instituted a New Covenant. Does this mean then that the disciple of Jesus could ignore or even discard the Law and the Prophets? Not at all. Jesus' followers continued to read and respect the Old Testament. But they read it in a new light. For Christians, the Old Testament can never be an end in itself. It is a sign pointing to Jesus, not the destination itself.

Picture a builder who agrees to construct a house for a customer. He signs a contract stating the price, the description of the house, and the date by which the project will be completed. A short time later, the contractor sends a foreman and crew to begin to work. They labor for several weeks and shortly before the deadline finish the house.

What effect did the foreman have on the contract? Did he abolish it? Not at all! He fulfilled its terms. Was the contract valid? It was valid as soon as the contractor signed it and remained valid all during the construction. If either party had reneged on the terms, the other could have used the contract in court. When did the contract cease to be valid? In one sense, it will always be valid as an accurate witness of the original agreement. But once its terms were fulfilled, they were no longer binding on the parties. Though both the contractor and the customer might use parts of the contract to form new agreements in the future, once finished, the purpose of the old document (covenant) stands completed.

In a similar way, Jesus fulfilled the Law and the Prophets. In their place, He offered a New Covenant. Some parts of the New Covenant are strikingly similar to the Old. Nevertheless, the Old is completed. Its purpose has been accomplished.

To claim to fulfill the Law and the Prophets was a radical statement for Jesus to make. Both He and those who heard His teachings knew the implications of such an assertion. From this would flow the six illustrations that complete the rest of Matthew 5. "But I say to you," He would declare repeatedly. He, and only He, had the authority to explain the law of God fully. His authority was absolute. His word was final. It still is!

Obedience: No Option

Only when the issue of Jesus' authority is understood do His words on obedience become clear (Matthew 5:19). The commandments that are to be practiced and taught and that determine one's status in the kingdom are not the commandments of the Law and the Prophets, but the commandments of the new kingdom. In Jesus' teachings lie the "will of [His] Father" (Matthew 7:21). It is these teachings that the wise man practices and the foolish man ignores (Matthew 7:24-27).

It is no accident that Matthew concludes his Gospel with words that so clearly summarize this same appeal to the absolute authority of Jesus' teachings:

> All authority in heaven and on earth has been given to me. Therefore go and make disciples of all nations, baptizing them in the name of the Father and of the Son and of the Holy Spirit, and teaching them to obey everything I have commanded you. And surely I am with you always, to the very end of the age (Matthew 28:18-20).

Beyond the Scribes and the Pharisees

This was the first principle Jesus wanted to make clear about the relationship of His kingdom to the Old Testament. He fulfilled, not destroyed, all that God had revealed. Next, Jesus taught that His kingdom was not to be confused with the practices and popular interpretations of the day. His kingdom was intimately related to everything the Law and the Prophets stood for and at the same time totally in opposition to the scribes and the Pharisees. That He could demand a righteousness that went beyond that of these two groups of religious experts was a shocking idea.

The Pharisees were a relatively small but vocal minority of fanatical Jews who were determined to obey God's law whether anyone else did or not. And most of the time, they were convinced that no one else did. Their origins are a bit uncertain. Most likely, the Pharisees evolved from a Jewish separatist faction during the Greek occupation three centuries before the time of Christ. The "separated ones" came to believe that Israel could be certain of the blessings of God only if the people were faithful to the smallest details of the law.

To insure this obedience, the Pharisees devoted themselves to preserving and protecting the law. This they did by developing an intricate system of interpretation that was designed to make adherance to the law certain by dividing it into smaller and smaller details and rules. These traditions, the "Mishnah" as they were called, contained six hundred thirteen rules. Two hundred forty-eight were commands and three hundred sixty-five (one for each day of the year) were prohibitions. The Mishnah included over thirty-nine separate Sabbath regulations alone.

While the Pharisees were largely middle class "laymen," the scribes were the professionals. They were doctors of theology and lawyers who specialized in the legal system of the rabbis. Together, the scribes and the Pharisees dominated the life of the synagogue, the center of every Jewish community. The Pharisees were the devoted lay leaders who wanted to live the traditions in the midst of a corrupt world. The scribes were the copiers, the teachers, and the official interpreters of the religious code.

The Righteousness of God

Like Jesus, the scribes and the Pharisees claimed to respect and obey the law. But there the similarities ended. For them, righteousness was a human activity. It involved observing the ceremonies and rituals of Moses to the letter. For Jesus, righteousness was first of all a right relationship to God. Devotion to God led the Pharisees to despise men and women who weren't quite as good as they thought they were. For Jesus, hunger for God resulted in love and compassion for sinners.

The very thing they thought bound them to God (the law and their traditions) actually separated the Pharisees and the scribes from enjoying full fellowship with Him. They were self-righteous, not God-righteous. They condemned others but stood condemned themselves. They set out to separate themselves from sinners and ended up separated from God.

Majoring in Minors

Jesus saw beyond the ritual and exposed the deep-seated "heart condition" of even the religious. In a series of scathing rebukes, He denounced their inconsistencies (Matthew 23:3) and self-centered religion (Matthew 23:5-12). They sought converts to their little empires but not to the kingdom of God (Matthew 23:13-15). Their expertise in the law became a tool to devise new ways to sin in the spirit while claiming obedience in the letter of the law (Matthew 23:16-22). They majored in minors and ignored the very things God desired in His people (Matthew 23:23, 24). They had become evangelists of Hell (Matthew 23:15), "blind guides" (Matthew 23:16), gnat-strainers and camel swallowers (Matthew 23:24), dirty cups (Matthew 23:25), painted tombs (Matthew 23:27), and prophet killers (Matthew 23:24).

To be totally fair to the record, we also must acknowledge that there were probably many sincere Pharisees and scribes who were honestly trying to please God. To most of their contemporaries, these religious leaders were living examples of righteousness. If they were excluded from the kingdom, who could be included?

Jesus knew what others didn't know. He knew that despite all of the law-keeping and rule-making, the scribes and Pharisees were really no different from anyone else. They were sinners like the publicans (tax-collectors) they so loudly condemned; their sins were just different. In fact, their self-righteousness made matters worse. Because they refused to acknowledge their problem, they rejected the very one who held the solution. That solution was a "greater righteousness." His kingdom was based not on keeping rules, but in living under the rule of God. The law of His kingdom and the resulting righteousness was written on the heart by the Spirit of God just as the prophets of old had promised (Jeremiah 31:31-34).

A Tale of Two Pharisees

The real-life experiences of two men, both Pharisees, help illustrate the nature of the kingdom and the righteousness Jesus demanded. Nicodemus came secretly to discover whether what he had heard about Jesus was true. He knew the Gallilean was more than his fellow Pharisees were willing to accept. Nicodemus was smart, morally upright, and devoutly religious. But he wasn't prepared for what Jesus would tell him.

"No one can see the kingdom of God," Jesus said, "unless he is born again" (John 3:3).

A greater righteousness! Born again! Jesus took the entrance to the kingdom of God and moved it beyond the reach of law-keepers and rule-makers. He placed it where only babies could enter!

By his own account, Pharisee number 2 was a "Hebrew of Hebrews." Paul's zeal for God and the law was second to none. He was a Pharisee who could claim absolute righteousness before the law (Philippians 3:4-6). But not before God!

When Paul met the resurrected Jesus, his entire perspective changed. After Ananias restored Paul's sight following the traumatic encounter on the Damascus road, the once-proud Pharisee saw something he had never seen before—his own sinfulness before God (Acts 9:1-19). The Jesus he had once hated became the one he loved more than anyone or anything else.

Paul's testimony explains the new kingdom righteousness announced by Jesus:

> But whatever was to my profit I now consider loss for the sake of Christ. What is more, I consider everything a loss compared to the surpassing greatness of knowing Christ Jesus my Lord, for whose sake I have lost all things. I consider them rubbish, that I may gain Christ and be found in him, not having a righteousness of my own that comes from the law, but that which is through faith in Christ—the righteousness that comes from God and is by faith. I want to know Christ and the power of his resurrection and the fellowship of sharing in his sufferings, becoming like him in his death, and so, somehow, to attain to the resurrection of the dead (Philippians 3:7-11).

Chapter Four

The Murder of the Spirit
Matthew 5:21-26

Throughout Jesus' ministry, He made two things very clear. First, He insisted that He came to fulfill the Law and the Prophets. From His first sermon in His hometown of Nazareth, to those intimate sea-side encounters with His disciples after the resurrection, His theme remained the same. "Everything must be fulfilled that is written about me" (Luke 24:44; cf. Luke 4:21).

Jesus also made it clear that many of the teachings and practices so popular among the religious leaders of His day were far from pleasing to God. Something was missing. His declaration that the "righteousness of the scribes and Pharisees" was not enough to insure entrance into the kingdom was a radical statement.

When Religion Turns Sour

In Matthew 23, Jesus unleashed a scathing expose of the false piety and perverted faith of the scribes and Pharisees. This diagnosis of their problem provides an important backdrop against which to view His statements in Matthew 5.

First, He said, they were stumbling blocks to the kingdom for those who truly wanted to know God (Matthew 23:13). According to Jesus, the Pharisees were determined that if they didn't make it to Heaven, no one would. The result was that they became evangelists of Hell (Matthew 23:15). They would go to any lengths to spread their traditions and distortions of God's law.

But their religious zeal became the occasion for greater and greater dishonesty (Matthew 23:16-22). They were so blind to the truth that they lost all sense of perspective. They majored in minors (Matthew 23, 24). They overlooked the great things of God in order to attend to details.

They had turned religion into an external show (Matthew 23:25, 26). Their faith was a deception. Beneath the appearance of life was a heart of death (Matthew 23:27, 28). This led them to a false pride in their heritage. They glorified God in the past tense while rejecting His spokesmen in the present (Matthew 23:29-36).

The Jesus Principles

In contrast, Jesus emphasized a totally different kind of religion. He didn't just add new laws or modify the old ones. His kingdom was entirely new, based on five fundamental truths:

First, God is interested in the heart, not just the conduct of people. Behavior matters, but it is not all that matters. God judges according to the spirit as well as the letter of the law. Jesus knew that man's heart condition was his real problem. From a man's inner spirit flows all the sin and evil that pollute his life. Change a man's heart, and you change the whole man.

Next, God's laws are a means to an end and not an end in themselves. The Pharisees had taken the Sabbath regulations and turned what had been a day of rest into a dreaded system of rules and regulations. "The Sabbath was made for man, not man for the Sabbath," Jesus reminded them (Mark 2:27). The goal of all of the law was to make men better lovers of God and of one another, not just better law-keepers.

Also, according to Jesus, obedience to God is essentially positive. The question is not what a person hasn't done, but what he has done. The deeds that matter most are the acts of love and mercy that reach out to a neighbor in need, not just abstaining from forbidden places or forbidden passions.

Next, Jesus insisted that the kingdom is a place of joy and peace. He hadn't come to burden men with more and bigger regulations. He came to set them free. Those most zealous for God's law often forgot that God's commandments were for their good always (Deuteronomy 6:24). His commands are never burdensome (1 John 5:3).

Finally, Jesus taught that no man can be good enough for God just by being good. The most flagrant sinner is closer to God when he cries out for mercy than a so-called righteous man worshiping in self-satisfied arrogance (Luke 18:9-14). Self-righteousness erects an impenetrable barrier between God and man.

The Windows of Heaven

Jesus illustrated the radical differences between His kingdom and the righteousness proclaimed by others with six illustrations

(Matthew 5:21-48). These six examples provide windows through which the inner righteousness of the kingdom can be seen. All six follow the same basic structure.

First, Jesus cited what His disciples had heard (Matthew 5:21, 27, 31, 33, 38, and 43). His reference was to the teachings of the rabbis that had been handed down from one generation to another and not to the law itself. If He had been citing Scripture, He would more likely have said, "You have heard that it was written." Instead, He said, "You have heard that it was said."

In each case, Jesus began with the customary understanding of God's Word and showed how its true intent and meaning went far beyond the accepted norms of the day. In none of the six examples did Jesus contradict the spirit or context of the Ten Commandments or other Old Testament teaching. Rather, He insisted that the very ones who defended the law so vigorously had denied and broken it again and again (cf. Mark 7:8, 9, 13).

In each illustration, Jesus set up a striking contrast. "You have heard," but "I say to you." He asserted His own authority. The rabbis' teachings were always based on someone else's authority. "Rabbi Shammai says this," or, "Rabbi Akbar says that."

A famous story from the first century concerning one of the most famous rabbis, Hillel, tells that he was once asked for a decision on a rather technical point of the law. The rabbi argued all day, carefully laying out his position. Despite his tightly reasoned case, his hearers refused to accept his conclusion.

Finally, he said, "I have received this tradition from Shemaiah and Abtalion" (two of the great leaders of the preceding generation). According to the story, the people immediately accepted the decision and voted Hillel their leader.

In contrast, Jesus cited no one. He simply said, "I say to you!" No wonder the crowds were amazed. "He taught as one who had authority, and not as their teachers of the law" (Matthew 7:29).

One-eyed Lusting

Jesus also used irony and exaggeration to press home the point of each illustration. This is important to note because much unnecessary confusion has resulted from attempts to take every one of Jesus' words literally. To do so can easily lead to the very artificial legalism that He was speaking against.

The clearest example of this is found in the second illustration (Matthew 5:27-30). If the problem of lust and moral offense is solved by gouging out one's eyes and cutting off one's hands, then the blind and the crippled must be at the front of the line for sainthood. Obviously not! A man can lust with one eye just as easily as with two. The problem is inside, not outside. Jesus' words must be taken seriously, as we will note. But to insist on taking every one literally may result in a disobedience even more distorted than that of the scribes and Pharisees.

Perhaps the most important lesson to note as we examine each of the illustrations is the central theme that runs throughout. Jesus began by insisting that He came to fulfill the Law and the Prophets. He concluded by declaring that the Law and the Prophets are summed up by love for others. Both Jesus and Paul would later declare that love for God and man was what the entire law was about (Matthew 22:36-40; Galatians 5:14). Each illustration of kingdom righteousness demonstrates this. Anger, lust, divorce, dishonesty, retaliation, as well as outright hatred are perversions of love. The exceeding righteousness of the kingdom and the perfect love of the child of God are one and the same.

"You Shall Not Murder"

Jesus began His explanation of kingdom conduct with an example based on the sixth commandment. "You shall not murder" was a fundamental part of God's covenant with Israel (Exodus 20:13; Deuteronomy 5:17). Centuries before, He had set forth the same principle for Noah and his children, who were to populate the freshly cleansed earth (Genesis 9:5, 6). Respect for human life was the bedrock upon which a new civilization could be built.

The penalty for intentionally taking an innocent life was death, the ultimate punishment that mankind can invoke against one of its own (Leviticus 24:21; Genesis 9:6). To argue, as some do today, that taking a life as punishment for murder is contradictory misses the point. If human life is sacred, then those who take it without justification must be given the severest punishment possible. To do less is to cheapen life. This assumes, however, that the punishment is meted out with the strictest seriousness and justice.

The criminal justice system of ancient Israel differed greatly from that found in most modern nations. Punishment was executed by relatives. These near kinsmen were officially responsible for seeing that justice was served. They were not self-appointed vigilantes, but were required to operate within the limits of the law. The detailed regulations are recorded in Numbers 35.

Old-fashioned Justice

According to the law, when a murder took place, the near kinsmen would immediately apprehend the offender. To protect the innocent, cities of refuge were established. The accused could seek asylum in these cities, where he could not be touched by the executioner until a trial had been held.

The proceedings took place before the local assembly of elders. If he was found guilty, the murderer was turned over to the "avenger of blood" for execution. However, if the investigation revealed that the death was accidental, the accused was protected from execution. Instead, he was returned to the city of refuge where he was forced to remain until the death of the next high priest. At that time, he was free to go. However, anytime he ventured outside of the designated city before the appointed time, he could be legally put to death by the avenger.

Two additional regulations insured fairness. First, no execution could take place without the testimony of two witnesses. Even one eye witness was not enough. Second, no one was allowed to purchase his freedom. The wealthy and the poor alike faced the same penalties.

Created in His Image

When Jesus said, "You have heard that it was said to the people long ago, 'Do not murder, and anyone who murders will be subject to the judgment,'" He was probably referring not so much to the Old Testament law against murder and the regulations for its punishment as to the legalistic perversions of it. The scribes and the Pharisees taught what the law said all right, but they ripped it from its context and gave it an emphasis much different from that originally found in the Ten Commandments. Viewed through their legalistic lenses, the original intention of the sixth commandment became warped and distorted.

They saw in the law nothing more than a prohibition against the act of killing. But the law was more than that. It was an effort to exhalt and protect the sacredness of human life. They reasoned that if they had not murdered anyone, they had fulfilled the commandment of God. They forgot that there is more than one way to cheapen life. Jesus reminded them.

The Pharisees also lost sight of the original motive behind the commandment. To say that a person should not commit murder because if he did, he would be forced to stand trial may have been true enough, but it missed the point of God's law altogether. The original motive for the law against murder was respect for God and the creation made in His image. Noah was told: "Whoever sheds the blood of man, by man shall his blood be shed; for in the image of God has God made man" (Genesis 9:6). The Israelites were told that bloodshed polluted the land and made it unfit for the presence of God among His people (Numbers 35:33-34). The fear of God, not just the fear of men, made respect for human life important.

The Larger Circle

Jesus extended the law against murder in four ways. First, He broadened its scope. "Anyone who is angry with his brother will be subject to judgment," He insisted. He left no room for self-righteousness. Anyone who had experienced anger stood outside God's will alongside the most notorious murderer.

The Pharisees happily drew a line that separated themselves from sinners. On the other side of the line were murderers and adulterers. Jesus, in effect, drew a circle that included all sinners, those who harbored violent attitudes as well as those who committed violent actions. Both groups were guilty before God.

But Jesus didn't stop there. He drew a second circle and offered pardon to anyone willing to step from sin into salvation. This step was impossible for all but those who were ready to admit their need of forgiveness.

Second, Jesus deepened the concern of the law. Instead of limiting the sixth commandment to the act of murder, Jesus pushed it to its most basic issue. The problem, according to Jesus, was the attitude and emotion behind the act. Anger was the real culprit. Violence and murder were by-products of an angry heart. The inner attitude, not just the outward act, made one a sinner.

The Bible uses two different words for *anger.* The difference between the two is only slight. The first is frequently translated "wrath." The original term was related to the Latin expression for smoke or steam. It described a sudden outburst of anger that boiled over into words or actions. The other term came from a root word that meant to become puffed up or excited. This word for anger often described a more deliberate attitude. The outburst may come suddenly, but it results from having harbored ill will until it finally breaks out into the open. It was this second term that is used in Matthew 5:22.

The Higher Law

Third, Jesus raised the demands of the law. He described the spirit that violates the sixth commandment in three stages. Anger comes first, then words. He cited two different expressions of contempt. The distinction is subtle at best. *Raca* literally meant "empty headed." It voiced ridicule for another's intelligence. *You fool* expressed contempt for another's character or heart. Both evidenced a mean-spirited disrespect for another human being.

The punishment for anger, Jesus said, was the same as for murder. The guilty party was subject to a trial before the local council. Calling someone an idiot *(Raca)* was a federal offense. The name-caller would face the Jewish supreme court, the Sanhedrin. But to label another a "fool" would lead to Hell itself.

At the very least, Jesus elevated the power of the tongue to its proper place. Children sing, "Sticks and stones may break my bones, but names will never hurt me." Adults know better! Harsh words can cut and maim like the sharpest sword (Proverbs 12:18). Hateful, inconsiderate words can kill a reputation and destroy a person's self-respect and confidence. A wounded spirit is much more difficult to mend than a broken leg.

Jesus' primary emphasis, however, lies in another area. To take His words literally could easily lead to an absurd legalism even worse than that of the scribes and the Pharisees. To worry about the difference between *Raca* and *you fool* is to miss the point altogether. Jesus wasn't suggesting that there are three different punishments for three different attitudes, one for anger, one for disrespect, and an altogether different one for contempt. In fact, Jesus was ridiculing the very kind of spiritual gymnastics that try to make such fine distinctions while all the time denying the very spirit of God's will.

Attempting to take Jesus' statement literally leaves a number of rather significant problems. For one thing, no human court, even the Sanhedrin, can make the inner judgments necessary to prosecute an attitude or emotion such as anger. Second, Jesus himself demonstrated anger at the stubborn unbelief of the very Pharisees He criticized here (Mark 3:5). On another occasion, He openly called them fools (Matthew 23:17). Surely, one cannot assume that Jesus did the very thing that He said would be punished in Hell. On the other hand, why does saying *you fool* deserve Hell while uttering a nearly synonomous term *Raca* only calls for the judgment of the supreme court? Jesus' admonition points to something far deeper than just the superficial meaning of the rules He set forth.

Away With Rules

The Pharisees were rule-makers and rule-keepers. They delighted in the kind of fine legal distinctions that Jesus seemed to suggest. Their thirty-nine Sabbath regulations provide the classic example of legalism gone wild. Given half a chance, they would have liked nothing better than to develop a whole new code of conduct based on the difference between *Raca* and *you fool.*

That was their problem. They were so infatuated with rule-making that they forgot the reason for God's rules. The point wasn't just that anger, insults, contempt, or even murder were evil. It was that love and respect for one's fellow man were so much better. Jesus exposed the absurdity of the negative, legalistic, "rule-making" approach to human relationships.

"You want rules?" He suggested. "I'll give you rules. But see where this kind of thinking will lead you? You may avoid murder, and even anger. But somewhere you'll still break a rule and end up no better off than you were with the one rule, 'You shall not murder!'"

Wanted: Peacemakers

This discussion leaves us with the fourth way Jesus extended the sixth commandment. If He had only broadened the meaning of the command and raised its requirements to include anger and insults, His words would not have been nearly as revolutionary as they were and still are. Instead of leaving the issue where the Pharisees and the modern legalists could argue about it and then ignore it, Jesus provided a positive alternative. Here lies the whole point of His illustration of kingdom righteousness.

God's will is not just that men and women refrain from murder. He isn't even satisfied when they control their tempers and bite their tongues. What He desires is love and mercy. He wants a kingdom of peacemakers.

Jesus offered one alternative to murder, anger, and insults: reconciliation/peacemaking! To explain what He meant, He provided two examples (Matthew 5:23-26). Both emphasize the priority of peacemaking.

The first shows that seeking reconciliation with a brother is more important than ritual or even worship. The story, of course, is set in the context of first-century Jewish life. A disciple who was in the very act of presenting a sacrifice (perhaps a peace offering) at the altar and remembered a problem with a brother was told to leave the gift and first make peace. He wasn't even to finish the sacrifice. Offerings can wait, but peace can't!

Centuries before, the prophet had reminded the people of Israel that God requires more than sacrifice. "He has showed you, O man, what is good. And what does the Lord require of you? To act justly and to love mercy and to walk humbly with your God" (Micah 6:8).

Something Better Than Justice

The second story demonstrates that peace-making is even more important than personal rights and justice. The first illustration took place on the way to church; the second, on the way to court. Here the believer is seeking relief from the judge against the demands of the adversary. He likely hopes to win the judge's favor or he wouldn't have let the matter go that far.

But Jesus calls for a concern bigger than one's own personal rights. Kingdom righteousness seeks reconciliation, not rights. In the story, Jesus offered a very practical reason for this radical behavior. It is possible that the court case might go in favor of the adversary. If that happens, everything could be lost.

How Shall We Then Live?

Jesus provided the only solution to the murder-anger-insult cycle. Biting our tongue, counting to ten, or turning and walking the other way when confronted with conflict will never do. Instead of fleeing conflict, Jesus calls us to walk right into the middle of it and to make peace.

That's tough! It's a lot easier to make up rules and lists of dos and don'ts. We can always delay our obedience by arguing over rules. But Jesus cuts clean through all of that.

Where do we start? First, we think of someone with whom we are having a personal problem. That doesn't take long. You have probably already been thinking of someone while you read these last few pages.

Next, go to him and seek peace.

What do you do when you get there?

Whatever it takes!

Chapter Five

The High Price of Purity
Matthew 5:27-30

Throughout His teachings, and especially in the Sermon on the Mount, Jesus performed major surgery on the popular morals of His day—and ours. Layer by layer, He stripped away the hypocrisy and false righteousness that had grown over God's law. He exposed the nerve of man's immorality. He focused the white light of truth on the darkest recesses of man's inner soul. In the process, He revealed once and for all the folly of claiming to be pure before God just because we have successfully hidden the truth from others.

Exceeding Righteousness

Each of Jesus' six illustrations of "exceeding righteousness" concentrates on a different area of human relationships. They call for a faith that lives in the world, not just in the cloistered sanctuary of a temple. All six illustrations build upon one another. And all six stand on three basic principles that form the foundation of Jesus' moral code.

1. *All of life is sacred.* Jesus allowed no sacred/secular division as is so popular in the modern world. Every issue, every relationship, is subject to His rule and lordship. A disciple dare not label certain parts of life "religious" and another part "private."

Most of us tend to become a bit uncomfortable with these illustrations from the Sermon on the Mount. It is one thing to talk about prayer and fasting. It is something else altogether to link the faith to personal issues like anger and lust. We are tempted to say, "Wait a minute. That's none of your business. Those parts of my life are strictly personal!" Such thinking won't work. All of life belongs to the king!

2. *People, not rituals, are the focus of true godliness.* The wrong-headed belief that attending to the right ceremonies will

somehow make up for sins in other areas of life has always been popular. The prophets reminded Israel that God wanted love, mercy, and justice, not just sacrifices (Isaiah 1:10-20; Amos 5:21-27). Jesus called the Pharisees into judgment because they ignored these "more important matters of the law" in order to attend to the ceremonial details (Matthew 23:23).

3. *All have sinned.* No one, not even the most religious, can claim to be totally innocent before the holy God. Anyone who does claim such perfect righteousness has either misunderstood the depth of God's law or is blind to his own shortcomings.

Jesus' emphasis on motives and inner attitudes makes this clear. If sin were just a matter of avoiding certain actions, true morality would be a much simpler matter. But since it is internal and not just a result of surroundings, we can't escape. Every place we go, every decision we face, and every relationship in which we are involved is a moral matter. No wonder we fail so often! The opportunities are unlimited!

Once we realize that all have sinned, we can head in one of two totally different directions. We can cast off all responsibility, rationalizing that since all sin, there is no need trying to do right. Or we can throw ourselves on the grace of God. By faith, we can claim Jesus' offer to replace our sin with His righteousness. When that happens, we don't suddenly become sinless. We are just forgiven! When a person becomes a Christian, his battles with sin don't end. If anything, they grow more intense. But the Christian has something new that he never had before. He has a new beginning and a new power. The Holy Spirit works from the inside out to lead the Christian step by step down the path of greater righteousness.

Adultery in the Heart

I have taken the time to outline these basic concepts because it is at Jesus' second illustration that the world has the greatest difficulty with the moral principles of Jesus. Most can see some logic to Jesus' words about anger, honesty, and love, but when He places lust and adultery in the same category, many abandon ship. The world simply does not understand the issues.

Former President of the United States Jimmy Carter learned this the hard way. When he consented to an interview for *Playboy* magazine during his Presidential campaign in 1976, he no doubt understood the risk involved. But he didn't expect the furor that resulted from one statement. Many conservative Christians questioned the propriety of his doing the interview at all. But the media picked up on what was no doubt an honest attempt on the part of the "born-again" leader to explain his personal convictions. Most reporters were aghast that Carter would confess that he had 'committed adultery many times in his heart." Such talk was nonsense to the ears of most non-Christians. But the President had simply applied the principles of Jesus to his own life and admitted that he, like every man, was a sinner before God.

Social Sexploitation

One doesn't need to be a sociologist to recognize the fact that our culture has a serious problem with Jesus' teachings on sex and lust. Sexploitation is everywhere! As I sat in my living room and watched television with my family last night, I saw everything from soap to beer to power saws marketed with sex. Soap operas, situation comedies, and talk shows all attempt to get as much mileage as possible from suggestive and sometimes outright adulterous situations. This was just network television. If my home had cable movie channels, which it doesn't and I hope never will, I could tune into an unlimited variety of sexsational programs.

Today, radio isn't much better. Much of contemporary rock and country music plays to the sexual fantasies and desires of its fans.

C. S. Lewis offers a stinging critique of our twentieth-century distortion of sex. "You can get a large audience together for a strip-tease act—that is, to watch a girl undress on stage. Now suppose you came to a country where you could fill a theatre by simply bringing a covered plate onto the stage and then slowly lifting the cover so as to let everyone see, just before the lights went out, that it contained a mutton chop or a bit of bacon. Would you not think that in that country something had gone wrong with the appetite for food? And would not anyone who had grown up in a different world think there is something equally queer about the state of the sex instinct among us?" *(Mere Christianity,* p. 75)

Everyone knows, but few of us are willing to admit, how rapidly the situation has worsened before our very eyes. Pornography, for example, has been widely tolerated, if not accepted, by most Americans at the same time it has become more and more degenerate. It provides a barometer of our society's declining morals.

During World War II, a scantily-clad model gracing the pages of a poster or calendar was of questionable taste. In the 1950's, *Playboy* came on the scene and complete nudity became the order of the day. Once desensitized, society quickly grew accustomed to the explicit sex and homosexuality of hard-core pornography. In the last ten years, photographs of bestiality between animals and women have become available at the neighborhood "adult" bookstore.

Today, child pornography or "kiddie porn" is the rage. Six- and seven-year-olds, and even tiny infants, are used in photographs and films of every perversion imaginable. In 1982, U.S. customs officials reported that from 1978-81, government agents had confiscated a quarter of a million pieces of pornography. Almost three-fourths of the illicit material involved children.

What's next? One thing is certain. It will get worse!

Denmark offers a graphic example of where America is headed. The Danish government first legalized pornography in 1967. Social planners argued that the relaxed atmosphere of toleration would cause a decline in sex crimes and other forms of emotional distress. In 1970, sex education was made mandatory. This was necessary, they reasoned, to give children the needed information with which they could make more mature decisions on their own.

Later, all "age of consent laws" were removed from the books in Denmark. Reports of sex crimes decreased throughout the nation. Not because the moral climate improved, but because the definitions had been changed. Homosexuality, statutory rape, sodomy, and indecent exposure all became "legal." In 1973, abortion on demand was legalized. Contraceptives were made available to anyone free of charge, regardless of age.

What has been the result of the rapid social change in Denmark. Sexual assault and rape has increased 300%. Venereal disease among adults has jumped 200%. Among those fifteen and under, venereal disease has accelerated by more than 400%! Abortions have multiplied by 500%. In six years, the divorce rate doubled and illegitimate pregnancies increased by 50%.

The Missing Commandment

In 1623, the English printing firm of Baker and Lukas published a Bible that quickly became known as the "Wicked Bible." Proofreaders had allowed to go unnoticed the fact that the "not" of Exodus 20:13 had been omitted. The text read, "Thou shalt commit adultery." Baker and Lukas were quickly fined and the whole edition destroyed.

A similar event has happened in the twentieth century. Today the "not" remains in the Bible. But it has been purged from society's standards of conduct. Charles Leroux, a columnist with the *Chicago Tribune,* observes that in the media "there are now nine commandments. The one about adultery is no longer operable."

Chastity has become the new embarrassment! John White, in his book *Eros Defiled,* laments the fact that new commandments have replaced the seventh—"Thou shalt not be jealous. Thou shalt not be possessive of thy wife or husband. Thou shalt always be understanding of the wonderful maturing process that thy husband is undergoing in his fascination with thy neighbor Mary."

Despite its promises of new-found freedom and pleasure, the sexual revolution has left many victims. A *Cosmopolitan* magazine survey of 106,000 Americans revealed that a majority of the women were disappointed with their sexual liberation. According to the report, "So many readers wrote negatively about the sexual revolution, expressing longings for vanished intimacy, and the now elusive joys of romance and commitment, that we began to sense that there might be a sexual counter-revolution under way in America."

Against such a backdrop of moral decay and spiritual desperation, the Bible's sensitive and realistic view of sexual morality has much to offer. Christians and non-Christians alike need to hear afresh Jesus' high call for moral purity.

The Sacredness of Sex

Jesus cited the seventh commandment as the second illustration of kingdom conduct (Exodus 20:14; Deuteronomy 5:18). In ancient Israel, such a trespass was punishable by death (Leviticus 20:10-16; Deuteronomy 22:22). As with His previous example, Jesus did not annul the law. He exposed the original meaning by placing it in its original context.

The real problem of adultery preceded the action. As with anger/murder, adultery begins with lust. This was not a new idea for those who knew the Old Testament. The tenth commandment made it clear, "You shall not covet your neighbor's wife" (Exodus

20:17). Job recognized the problem when he insisted that he had "made a covenant with my eyes not to look lustfully at a girl" (Job 31:1). Statements similar to Jesus' can be found in the writings of the first-century rabbis.

Despite what should have been a well-understood principle, some in Jesus' day still failed to grasp the full implications of the seventh commandment. The prohibition against adultery became limited in two ways:

First, the act was separated from the thought. Adultery was a sin; adulterous thinking was not. Second, adultery was primarily a sin committed against a husband. A double standard existed in Greek, Roman, and even Jewish societies. While a man was free to have mistresses and concubines, a wife was expected to remain faithful to one husband. Even a man who raped a woman was not condemned for sinning against the woman, but because of his sin against the husband if she was married or against the father if she was not (Deuteronomy 22:22-29). Technically, a man could commit adultery only if a married (or betrothed) woman was involved.

A Word From the Creator

To appreciate fully both the spirit of the Old Testament and intent of Jesus' ethic, we need to see more clearly the Bible's total view of sex. Many distortions result from separating the Bible's commandments about sexual behavior from their context. One thing is obvious: the Bible is not prudish about sex. It talks openly and candidly concerning both the positive and negative aspects of human sexuality.

Unfortunately, those who claim allegiance to the Scriptural standards have not always shared the same attitude. Queen Victoria held such a distorted attitude toward anything remotely related to sex that she ordered books authored by male and female writers to be separated in the royal library!

The first truth that the Bible teaches about sex is that it was created by God. Sex was not the original sin. God made mankind male and female. In the context of a committed and loving marriage, sex is a beautiful gift of God. Nothing about it contradicts the call to holiness and righteousness (Hebrew 13:4; 1 Corinthians 6:18-20).

Scripture also insists that *God created sex for a purpose*. He designed it for reproduction (Genesis 1:28), to develop intimacy between husband and wife (Genesis 2:24, 25), and for pleasure. Both the husband and the wife are entitled to the experience of sexual fulfillment (1 Corinthians 7:2-5).

Unfortunately, many have difficulty conceiving of a God who actually intends that husband and wife enjoy the pleasures of sex. Too many resemble the boy described by C. S. Lewis, who defined God as "the sort of person who is always snooping around to see if anyone is enjoying himself and trying to stop it." Simply remembering that God created male and female and then saw that "it was very good" (Genesis 1:31) should dispel such thinking forever.

The Bible also teaches that *sex can be abused and misused.* In the proper context and with the necessary love, sex is a powerful, life-sustaining force. Distorted, it ruins lives and families without mercy.

Scripture is honest in its portrayal of sexual sin. Some of the Old Testament's greatest heroes fell victim to its wiles. David (2 Samuel 11), Samson (Judges 16), Solomon (1 Kings 11), Shechem (Genesis 34), and Judah (Genesis 38) all experienced the judgment of God in one form or another because of their transgressions involving misused sex. Scripture neither glosses over this evil nor dwells on it. Sexual sin is presented as a fact of life with which the child of God must deal.

The New Testament uses two key words for sexual sin. *Adultery* describes unlawful intercourse with the spouse of another (Mark 7:21; Luke 18:11; 1 Corinthians 6:9; Hebrews 13:4). Those guilty of it will not inherit the kingdom of God. Yet it is forgivable (1 Corinthians 6:9-11).

Fornication (KJV) or *sexual immorality* (NIV) is a more general term than adultery. It refers to any illicit sexual relationship. It sometimes includes adultery and at other times is distinguished from it (Mark 7:21; Matthew 15:19). Fornication is one of the marks of the old life of the flesh, from which Christians have been redeemed (Galatians 5:19; Ephesians 5:3; Colossians 3:5; 1 Thessalonians 4:3).

Third, the Bible teaches that *sex can be controlled.* It totally rejects the notion that the sex drive is an overwhelming force that pushes a man or woman to do things totally against one's will. However, Scripture does recognize the difficulty of self-control and cautions believers to remember their vulnerability (1 Corinthians 7:1-6).

55

The Heart: Adultery's Birthplace

Jesus countered the distortions and abuses of the seventh commandment with a bold declaration, "Anyone who looks at a woman lustfully has already committed adultery with her in his heart" (Matthew 5:28). His words bear three important lessons.

First, He reminded His disciples of what was already common knowledge. Sin, including adultery, is more than an act. It is first of all an attitude. The birthplace of adultery is not a brothel or even the bedroom. It begins in a willing heart.

The lustful look that Jesus describes is more than an appreciative glance at a woman. The grammar of the original language depicts it as (1) a continually looking (2) at a particular woman (3) for the purpose of lust. It is the look of a person who would commit the act if the occasion arose.

Socially, lust and adultery are two totally different issues. Adultery involves another person; lust takes place in the mind and heart of an individual. No one else is actually involved or hurt. But Jesus insisted that while there may be a clear social difference, morally, lust of the eye equals adultery of the heart. Since God judges the heart (1 Samuel 16:7), secret adultery transgresses His will for man.

The Life Cycle of Lust

James made it clear that lust is never a dead-end street. It always leads to death (James 1:13-15). Lust first is conceived in the heart. When developed, it gives birth to sin of every description. Full grown, what began as private lust leads to wars, conflicts, and ultimately death (James 4:1). No wonder Jesus warned of the danger of illicit desires as well as immoral behavior.

A Man's Sin, Too

Jesus also insisted that adultery is a male problem, not just a female issue. According to the popular Jewish thinking, adultery was a sin against a *husband*. A Jewish man was free to do whatever he pleased as long as he didn't involve a married or betrothed woman. Jesus placed the act and the attitude in an entirely different category. Anyone who looks with lusts stands condemned.

Paying the Price for Purity

Third, Jesus warned of the high price a person must be willing to pay if he or she wants to remain free of lust. He calls for radical surgery if necessary to maintain one's spiritual and moral health. "If your right eye causes you to sin, gouge it out and throw it away." "If your right hand causes you to sin, cut it off and throw it away."

These are strong actions! The phrase "cause to sin" literally referred to the trigger of a trap. Some translations use the word "stumblingblock." Jesus referred to the "right eye" and the "right hand" because most people considered the right side of the body the most vital. We use the similar expression today when someone says, "I'd give my right arm for that."

What did Jesus mean with these graphic expressions? As has been noted earlier, to take the words literally leads to all sorts of distortions. There have been those who have attempted to do exactly what Jesus said or more. Origin, a fourth-century Christian leader from Alexandria, had himself castrated in the misdirected belief that he was insuring his faithfulness to God.

The biggest problem with a literal obedience to Jesus' directive is that it doesn't help. A left-eyed man can lust just as easily as a fully-sighted man. A blind person may not be able to "look lustfully," but he can surely commit adultery in his heart. The true intent of Jesus' words must lie elsewhere.

Jesus emphasized two truths. First, His words may be a parody of the Pharisees' legalism. They tried to solve every moral dilemma with an external solution. Here He drove their legalism to an extreme and showed that even then the real source of the problem remained untouched. If the adultery is in the heart, simply removing the eye or the hand changes very little.

But probably more than this, Jesus was simply reminding His listeners that they must be willing to pay any price, make any sacrifice, if they are serious about moral purity. To do anything less is simply to toy with sin.

Edward Hastings tells of an English officer who was traveling with a native servant through the jungles of India. Suddenly, without warning, the servant cried out and in one quick move pulled a long dagger from his belt and slashed it down on his own outstretched hand. The officer watched in horror as his servant completely severed his hand.

"Are you mad?" he cried.

The servant pointed fearfully to a huge snake swiftly disappearing into the brush and then fainted.

The officer carefully wrapped the stump of his beloved companion. Eventually, the servant recovered. But when the dismembered hand was examined, it bore the deep marks of a cobra bite. Had the Indian not performed the apparent act of self-mutilation, he would have died within minutes. He lived only because he was willing to pay the price.

God takes sin seriously. We are tempted to treat it as a minor problem that only calls for minor solutions. Most of us are willing to take any necessary steps to achieve righteousness if the detour doesn't take too long or inconvenience us too much. Jesus considered sin such a problem that the cross was the only sufficient solution!

Holiness is God's will. He has left no doubt about that. "God did not call us to be impure, but to live a holy life. Therefore, he who rejects this instruction does not reject man but God, who gives you his Holy Spirit" (1 Thessalonians 4:7, 8)

Getting Serious About Sin

What price are you willing to pay to defeat sin? If removing an eye or cutting off a hand were enough, would you do it? What if overcoming sin required changing some habits? Would you be willing to stop reading certain books or viewing certain movies? What about seeking a different group of companions if necessary? No one can tell you exactly what price you may need to pay to walk in purity. One thing is certain. Whatever the cost, it's a bargain. The price of holiness can get awfully high; but the wages of sin is death!

When it's a choice between an eye and a hand or Hell, the choice should be clear. "It is better," Jesus insisted, "to lose one part of your body than for your whole body to go into hell" (Matthew 5:30). Hell is a serious matter; so is holiness!

Putting Sin to Death

Paul provides an explanation of the path to purity when he outlines five rules for holy living in Colossians 3:1-17.

1. Set your sights high. Remember that as a Christian, you have been set free from sin's power. Live up to your potential by concentrating on where you are headed (Colossians 3:1-4).

2. Bury the dead. The old you died with Christ. Don't try to carry the corpse. Put it in the grave along with all its old habits (Colossians 3:5-7).

58

3. Throw away the rags. A child of a king shouldn't wear the old garments of sin—anger, rage, malice, slander, and filthy language. He shouldn't even keep them in his closet. He doesn't need them anymore (Colossians 3:8-11).

4. Put on your Sunday-best. Christ provides an entirely new wardrobe for His family. A person should dress for the occasion when preparing to meet a king. "Clothe yourselves with compassion, kindness, humility, gentleness and patience (Colossians 3:12-14).

5. Honor the king. Holiness is not just a matter of keeping a few, or even many, rules. It requires living completely under the rule of God. That rule calls for making His will, His Word, and His honor number one in our lives (Colossians 3:15-17).

Looking for a King

In John Milton's classic story *Paradise Regained,* he retells the account of Jesus' temptations. In the scene where Satan calls for Jesus to turn the stones into bread, Milton has the tempter challenge the Savior to act like a king.

"A king shouldn't go hungry," he says. "You're a king. You deserve to be treated like one. Do something about it."

Jesus resists and reminds the tempter, "He is truly a king who rules his own spirit."

Two men from the Old Testament demonstrate the truth of these words. Both were kings, but only one "ruled his own spirit." Each encountered similar temptations. But they faced the temptation in totally different ways.

King David saw, lusted, and acted (2 Samuel 11:1-5). What he wanted he took. He seduced Bathsheba and then arranged for the murder of her husband when all his attempts to cover the crime failed. After he thought the secret was secure, he discovered what he should have known all along. God knew! David and his family paid a high price for his lustful look.

Joseph, soon to become second only to the Pharoah, was a king inside and out (Genesis 39:1-20). When he was confronted with the advances of his master's wife, he resisted because he knew his sin would be "against God" (Genesis 39:9). Joseph knew enough to "flee fornication" (1 Corinthians 6:18, KJV). He paid a price for his purity, but he remained a true king even in prison.

It's Never Too Late to Change

Lust and adultery are serious sins in God's eyes. But they, too, can be forgiven. Every sinner who thinks he has gone too far to turn back needs to read Paul's words:

> Do not be deceived: Neither the sexually immoral nor idolators nor adulterers nor male prostitutes nor homosexual offenders nor thieves nor the greedy nor drunkards nor slanderers nor swindlers will inherit the kingdom of God. And that is what some of you were. But you were washed, you were sanctified, you were justified in the name of the Lord Jesus Christ and by the Spirit of our God" (1 Corinthians 6:9-11).

Chapter Six

What God Has Joined Together
Matthew 5:31, 32

Jesus' third illustration of "exceeding righteousness" was as emotionally-laden a topic in His day as it is in ours. Divorce is not a theoretical issue. It reaches to the very heart of our most intimate personal relationship. By including this in His examples of kingdom concerns, Jesus teaches that in marriage, as in all areas, of life, the disciple must "seek first his [God's] kingdom and his righteousness" (Matthew 6:33).

The discussion of divorce appropriately stands where it does in the list of six examples. Before and after the discussion of divorce, Jesus outlined two principles that would prevent the breakup of many marriages. First, a lust-free mind eliminates the seeds of unfaithfulness that destroy the marriage relationship. God's desire is for emotional and mental, as well as sexual, fidelity. Second, Jesus calls for absolute integrity. A person's verbal commitments should be sacred. Certainly, this includes marriage covenants. In these two issues, sexual purity and verbal integrity, Jesus provided the proper framework within which marriage and divorce must be discussed.

Danger: Proceed With Caution

I am aware that any discussion of divorce must be approached with extreme care. Some months ago, I and the other elders of the congregation where my family were worshiping at the time spent several weeks laboring with this delicate topic. We studied the Scriptures together, attempted to develop some strategies for applying the Scriptures in our ministries, and prayed for the wisdom and courage to carry out what we had learned. I think I can speak for all of us when I say that we came to two conclusions.

First, the Bible does speak to the issue. Where it speaks, we are obligated to obey that teaching individually and corporately.

Second, applying those teachings redemptively in the mixed-up world of the twentieth century is a very difficult and sometimes costly process. The problem is to remain compassionate with the people for whom we care and consistent with the Word of God. If that burden doesn't bring every Christian leader to his knees before the grace of God, nothing will! Two dangers confront us today as we seek to understand the Lord's teachings on divorce. First, the magnitude of the problem tempts us to modify our beliefs to make them more palatable to people. But public opinion polls should not determine doctrine. Scripture, and nothing less, must be our standard.

The governments of Jesus day did not record divorce statistics for history. If they had, I am confident that their figures would have been small compared to ours. Consider the divorce figures for the last century in this country alone:

Year	Marriages	Divorces	Rate Per 1,000 Population
1900	709,000	55,751	.7
1920	1,274,476	170,505	1.6
1940	1,595,879	264,000	2.0
1950	1,667,231	385,144	2.6
1960	1,523,000	393,000	2.2
1970	2,158,802	708,000	3.5
1980	2,413,000	1,182,000	5.2
1981	2,438,000	1,219,000	5.3
1982	2,495,000	1,180,000	5.1
1983	2,444,000	1,179,000	5.0
1984	2,487,000	1,155,000	4.9
1985	2,425,000	1,187,000	5.0

Divorce rates in proportion to the total population actually decreased in 1986 to the lowest figure since 1975 (4.8 per 1,000). But the ratio of divorces to marriages continues to hover alarmingly close to the fifty percent level. Two groups, the previously divorced and teenagers, are especially likely to divorce. Over half of all second marriages end in divorce. The rate for those who marry in their teens is twice as high as for those who marry in their late twenties. In the United States, divorce is a $3 billion-a-year industry.*

---

*Figures from The World Almanac (1986 and 1987).

More Than Numbers

Statistics don't tell the whole story. Behind every number are at least two people, their families, friends, and often their children, who have been deeply hurt by what has happened. Over five hundred thousand children live in single-parent families because of divorce. Almost every family and certainly every church has been touched by the problem in one way or another.

This creates a second danger for the church. On the one hand, we are tempted to make our teachings more acceptable. On the other hand, we are pressured to allow pastoral expediencies to determine doctrine rather than allowing the teachings of Scripture to dictate how we approach congregational problems. The church must be concerned about the plight of the divorced. The formerly married and the remarried need the gospel as everyone else. They need the loving support and care of God's people. But they also deserve to be taught the Word of God as it stands. Too often, preachers and elders compromise at the very point where they need to be most clear.

Lewis Smedes voiced this concern appropriately in an interview that appeared in the *Wittenburg Door.* "I think compassion has become synonymous with moral indifference in the churches today. In a mad dash to replace judgment with healing, we've forgotten that Jesus says, 'God doesn't want you to get a divorce ever.'" The Bible scholar and counselor further cautioned, "The church that simply says, 'we accept you' without saying 'we forgive you' is ignoring the reality of what's happened. A covenant has been violated. Someone has been hurt" (August/September, 1979, p. 14).

For the child of the kingdom, Jesus' words must settle the issue once and for all. Applying them may not be easy, but understanding must always be the first step.

You Have Heard: Keep It Legal

Jesus begins the third example with another quotation, "It has been said, 'Anyone who divorces his wife must give her a certificate of divorce.'" As with the other illustrations, this was a reference not to the Old Testament but to the popular views of the day. Jewish believers of the first century were confronted with two contradictory ideas about divorce. Both claimed to be based on the same Old Testament text.

Let's read that text and examine the rabbis' interpretations:

If a man marries a woman who becomes displeasing to him because he finds something indecent about her, and he writes her a certificate of divorce, gives it to her and sends her from his house, and if after she leaves his house she becomes the wife of another man, and her second husband dislikes her and writes her a certificate of divorce, gives it to her and sends her from his house, or if he dies, then her first husband, who divorced her, is not allowed to marry her again after she has been defiled. That would be detestable in the eyes of the Lord. Do not bring sin upon the land the Lord your God is giving you as an inheritance (Deuteronomy 24:1-4).

This passage was approached in two different ways by two different rabbinic schools. Rabbi Shammai concentrated on the phrase "something indecent" and concluded that the law taught that a man could divorce his wife if she were unfaithful to him. Rabbi Hillel emphasized "displeasing to him," teaching that a divorce could be obtained for almost any offense. "For any and every reason" was the way the Pharisees summarized this more liberal approach to divorce (Matthew 19:3).

In actual practice, such offenses could be as minor as burning the husband's dinner. Rabbi Akiba, another interpreter of the law, went even further. He said that a man could properly obtain a divorce if he found another woman that was more pleasing to him. The Jewish historian Josephus claims that the views of Hillel and Akiba were the most widely accepted in the first century.

Divorce: a Husband's Prerogative

While the rabbis differed on what constituted sufficient grounds for a divorce, they agreed on three other important matters. In Jewish society, only the man could initiate a divorce. A wife had no say in the matter. Second, divorce was a right of the husband. He need only have a reason. Finally, all sides in the debate considered divorce totally proper and moral as long as it was conducted legally.

A legal divorce required only that a written document, signed by at least two witnesses, be personally given to the wife. At that point, she had to leave the home. A judge and lawyer need not be involved. While the exact written form of a divorce document in Biblical times is unknown, samples of decrees from later periods have been found. One reads:

On the _____ day of the week _____ in the month _____ in the year _____ from the beginning of the world, according to the common computation in the province of _____ I _____ the son of _____ by whatever name I may be known, of the town of _____ with entire consent of mind, and without any constraint, have divorced, dismissed and expelled thee _____ daughter of _____ by whatever name thou art called, of the town _____ who hast been my wife hitherto; But now I have dismissed thee _____ the daughter of _____ by whatever name thou art called, of the town of _____ so as to be free at thy own disposal, to marry whomsoever thou pleasest, without hindrance from any-one, from this day for ever. Thou art therefore free for anyone [who would marry thee]. Let this be thy bill of divorce from me, a writing of separation and expulsion, according to the law of Moses and Israel.

_____ , son of _____ , witness

_____ , son of _____ , witness

(*International Standard Bible Encyclopedia*, II, Eerdmans, p. 865)

Deuteronomy 24: a Second Look

A closer look at Deuteronomy 24:1-4 reveals the problem with the popular interpretations. This was not really a divorce law at all! It said nothing about the grounds for divorce or who should or should not be given a divorce. The rabbis read the passage in the same way as did the translators of the King James Version. The KJV inserts two "If/then" statements in the regulation:

1. If a man finds something displeasing in his wife, then he should give her a written document of divorce (vs. 1).

2. If she marries another, then the first husband cannot take her back (vss. 2-4).

Look at the passage again in the New International Version. There is only one "If/then" rule: *If* a man marries a woman *and* he finds something displeasing in her *and* he gives a certificate of divorce *and* she remarries, *then* he may not remarry her.

This law assumed divorce; it did not prescribe it. In fact, the legal procedure was also assumed. All that this law did was to make permanent any divorce that took place. It offered protec-tion to a wife from being forced to remarry her former husband. Divorce became a matter that a man could not take lightly.

What did the "something unclean" that the rabbis debated so forcefully really mean? Unfortunately, we are in no better position to understand it than they were. The Hebrew phrase (which literally meant "the nakedness of the thing") is used in only one other place in the Old Testament (Deuteronomy 23:14). There Israel was told to observe certain procedures for disposing of human waste so that the Lord would not see "anything indecent" among the people.

The best we can do is determine some things it didn't mean:

1. It didn't mean adultery. The law was clear that proven adultery was to be punished by death, not divorce (Leviticus 20:10; Deuteronomy 22:22-27).

2. It didn't mean suspected adultery. Another law provided the procedure for that situation as well (Numbers 5:11-31).

3. It could not have been the discovery that a new bride was not a virgin as she had claimed. Here, too, the punishment was death by stoning (Deuteronomy 22:25-27).

The cause of the displeasure must have been something other than infidelity, but yet something significant enough to bring shame to the husband. The argument between Shammai and Hillel, however, missed the whole point of the text. They debated whether a husband could properly divorce his wife for one reason or another. Either way, Deuteronomy 24:1-4 was silent. It spoke to a totally different issue.

What God Has Joined

With this in the background, we are now in a position to hear the kingdom principle on divorce. "But I tell you," Jesus said, "that anyone who divorces his wife, except for marital unfaithfulness, causes her to become an adulteress, and anyone who marries the divorced woman commits adultery" (Matthew 5:32).

In this and the other passages where Jesus speaks to the issue of divorce (Matthew 19:1-12; Mark 10:1-12; Luke 16:18), He revealed six principles, each of which stands in stark contrast to the commonly held views of the scribes and Pharisees.

Jesus insisted that God's will was that married couples should not divorce. Later in His ministry, the Pharisees attempted to trap Jesus into siding with either Hillel or Shammai over the divorce issue (Matthew 19:1-12; Mark 10:1-12). The Pharisees asked the typical legal question, "Is it lawful for a man to divorce his wife for any and every reason?" To what must have been their surprise,

Jesus didn't appeal to Deuteronomy 24:1-4. He pointed them to the only text in the books of Moses that answered the question.

> "Haven't you read," he replied, "that at the beginning the Creator 'made them male and female,' and said, 'For this reason a man will leave his father and mother and be united to his wife, and the two will become one flesh'? So they are no longer two, but one. Therefore what God has joined together, let man not separate" (Matthew 19:4-6).

Simply to debate the proper grounds for divorce, Jesus insisted, was to miss the larger issue. Marriage was a divine act. Two people were made one by God. Divorce is to tear apart what God put together. It can never be reduced to a technical point of law.

Next, Jesus pointed out that Moses *permitted* divorce. He did not *command* it as the Pharisees contended (Matthew 19:7, 8). In Mark's summary of the same discussion, the wording has led some Bible scholars to conclude that Jesus also believed that Moses commanded divorce. He asked the Pharisees, "What did Moses command you?" (Mark 10:3). However, when the Pharisees responded by referring to Deuteronomy 24, Jesus immediately turned their attention to Genesis 1:27 and 2:24. Again, Jesus insisted that the only "law" in the Old Testament that spoke to the issue of divorce was in Genesis, not Deuteronomy. The reason that Moses permitted divorce was the sinfulness of the Israelites. As we have noted, the law of Deuteronomy 24 simply regulated an already existing situation. It offered a limited amount of protection to the wife while serving notice on the husband that divorce was not a matter to be taken lightly. If husbands and wives had followed God's plan, the divorce question would never have come up. It was a result of man's sin, not God's law.

The Broken Covenant

Jesus also taught that there is only one legitimate justification for a marriage partner ever to divorce the other—fornication (Matthew 5:32; 19:9). Under any other circumstances, if one or the other partner marries again after the divorce, that second marriage is adultery.

This immediately raises the question; what is fornication? Simply defined, fornication referred to any sexual sin. Originally, the Biblical term came from a word that meant "to sell." It described the prostitute, male or female, who performed sexual favors for a price. Technically, adultery was defined as unfaithfulness to the marriage covenant.

In modern law, fornication refers to sexual misconduct by the unmarried and adultery to that committed by the married. This strict distinction, however, did not exist in Bible times. Ezekiel (16:32-36), Jeremiah (3:8-9), and Hosea (3:1-3) all speak of Jehovah's "marriage" to Israel being defiled by the fornication of the people. *Fornication* was used figuratively for the sins of the people. But it was the sins of those who were "married" to God in a solemn covenant. "I gave faithless Israel her certificate of divorce and sent her away because of all her adulteries.... Because Israel's *immorality* [fornication] mattered so little to her, she defiled the land and committed adultery with stone and wood" (Jeremiah 3:8, 9).

Another ancient Jewish document (this one in Greek) indicates a similar relationship between fornication and adultery. Sirach 23:23 tells of a wife who "committed adultery by fornication."

In Luke 16:18 and Mark 10:11, 12, Jesus omits the "except for fornication" phrase and simply says that whoever "divorces his wife and marries another commits adultery." The reason for the different wording is unclear. Possibly, the statements in Mark and Luke can be understood against the background of the Jewish law where marital unfaithfulness was punished by death. That this was still the occasional practice in the time of Jesus can be seen from the occasion of the woman caught in adultery who was brought to Jesus by those who were about to stone her. When adulterers were punished in this way, there was no need for divorce because of fornication.

Jesus also taught that the husband and the wife were both subject to the same standard (Mark 10:11, 12). This was a revolutionary concept for most Jewish men. Men and women lived under two totally different sets of rules as far as first-century Jewish society was concerned. Jesus eliminated the double standard.

Man and Woman for Life

Jesus further taught that remarriage following a divorce for any other reason than fornication was adultery. The sexual relationship between a husband or a wife and another partner was a breech of the original covenant despite the fact that a divorce had been given and a new covenant established. God's standard was simple: one man and one woman for life. Anything less was contrary to His will.

Matthew 5:32 creates a problem for some. Jesus says, 'Anyone who divorces his wife, except for marital unfaithfulness, causes her to become an adulteress." The problem is the passive voice of the verb Jesus used. The best possible solution is found in the background of the day.

Given the social and economic realities of the first century, it was safe to assume that every divorced woman would remarry. She had little choice. Jesus placed the responsibility for her predicament squarely on the shoulders of the husband who divorced her despite the fact that she had remained faithful to him.

Some scholars have sought to explain the wording by claiming that the husband made the wife to appear to be an adulteress in the eyes of the community by divorcing her. This is unlikely given the lenient attitudes toward divorce in that day. Also, the fact that the man who marries the divorced woman is said to commit adultery makes it clear that Jesus is not just referring to public opinion, but to the actual breaking of a marriage covenant.

It is dangerous to press Jesus' words beyond what they actually say. However, two observations can be safely implied. The divorcing husband is no more free to remarry than the wife he sent away. On the other hand, a husband or wife who divorces because of fornication is apparently free to remarry without the new marriage being adulterous. Any other interpretation empties the passage of any meaning.

Finally, Jesus shifts the center of discussion away from the argument over the grounds for divorce and moves it toward God's positive purpose for marriage. Jesus does offer a legitimate basis for divorce, but that is not the primary matter. Many discussions of this topic become sidetracked at the same point the Pharisees went wrong. Some spend their time trying to discover the conditions under which divorce is legal. Jesus spent His time emphasizing the fact that God wants a husband and wife to be one flesh.

An Additional Word

One other passage of Scripture adds important insights into this topic. In 1 Corinthians 7:10-16, Paul offers guidance for believers who were wrestling with marriage problems.

To Christians married to Christians (1 Corinthians 7:10, 11) he applies Jesus' words. They are not to divorce. If they do, they must not remarry. He offers a very important reason. They must be free to be reconciled to their Christian mates.

To Christians married to non-Christians (1 Corinthians 7:12-16) he offers different advice. This time, he insists that his teachings are not founded on the words of Jesus, since they speak to a situation not covered by the Lord. This apostolic command, however, was no less authoritative. He was God's spokesman.

In a mixed marriage, the Christian was not to initiate a divorce. If the non-Christian, however, decided to leave, the Christian mate was not to try to prevent it. Under those conditions, the Christian mate was "not bound." The reason again is important. God has called Christians to live at peace, not to try to force a mate to keep a marriage together despite his or her will.

Bible scholars are divided over the exact implications of the phrase "not bound." Most likely, it implies that the Christian who has been abandoned by the non-Christian is free from any and all obligations to the original marriage covenant. This includes the freedom to remarry, but only to a Christian. The freedom to remarry squares with Paul's insistence that a Christian who has lost a mate to death should consider marriage lest he be tempted to commit sexual sin (1 Timothy 5:14; 1 Corinthians 7:8, 9).

Divorce and the Church Today

What do the words of Jesus say to the modern church? This is no small question. In the final analysis, every congregation and each group of elders must wrestle with these teachings and the implications for their people. A few observations may prove helpful in this process.

First, the church must emphasize the Biblical concept of marriage. Marriage must be seen as a serious commitment that is intended to last a lifetime and not just a passing phase from which one can escape when the first hint of trouble develops. This teaching needs to begin in the home and with small children. Premarital counseling and instruction becomes critical.

Next, the church must be willing to pay a price if it intends to teach what Jesus taught. In an age of compromise, many will not like to be told that divorce is wrong. The disciples' reaction clearly indicates that Jesus' teaching created no less a problem for those in the first century (Matthew 19:10).

A church that wants to act responsibly cannot be satisfied with just denouncing easy divorce. The leadership of the church must be willing to intervene, with loving support, in the lives of members whose marriage is failing. In some cases, this will simply mean providing competent counseling. In other cases, church discipline (Matthew 18:15-20) may need to be exercised. The leaders of churches who fail to bring a strong word of exhortation to members who divorce their Christian mates contrary to the clear teachings of Scripture or who refuse to work for reconciliation multiply the problem by their silence.

The church must also be willing and ready to provide practical help to those who need it. Financial support, child-care, and employment help are all issues faced especially by newly-divorced wives. Genuine faith and love find ways to meet needs wherever they are.

The church must always remember that divorce is not an unforgivable sin. This does not make it right. It simply means that if repented of, wrongful divorce can be forgiven just as any other sin. Must a divorced person who has remarried abandon that second marriage in order to receive that forgiveness? Nothing in Scripture would suggest that such a compounding of wrong would solve anything. Nevertheless, genuine repentance must take place. Wrongful divorce cannot be glossed over. To do so rejects the very authority of Jesus!

Building Quality Marriages

Finally, the church needs to demonstrate a genuine concern for the quality of Christian marriages. Many Christians and non-Christians first consider divorce because of the terrible condition of their marriage relationship. The best solution to this problem is not to wait until marriages are falling apart to offer help, but to provide on-going, preventative care for the marriage relationship. Local leaders must find the best ways to accomplish this in their congregations.

Chrysostom, the great fourth-century preacher, linked the Beatitudes to these words of Jesus about marriage and divorce: "For he that is meek, and a peacemaker, and poor in spirit, and merciful, how shall he cast out his wife? He that is used to reconciling others, how shall he be at variance with her that is his own?"

In the final analysis, marriage and family relationships provide the most accurate test of the genuineness of one's faith. Because of that fact, a good marriage and family is the gospel's most powerful witness.

71

Chapter Seven

The Great Divorce
Matthew 5:33-48

As serious as is the break-up of marriages and families, the contemporary church faces another divorce problem that is ultimately more dangerous. For lack of a better term, I'll call it "spiritual divorce."

Spiritual divorce is the separation of faith and life. Like its marital counterpart, spiritual divorce seeks to tear assunder what God has joined together. It splits religion and morals. It rips ethics and Christian living from any meaningful contact with business, politics, or any other relationships of daily life.

This is the great divorce of our day! It seeks to compartmentalize faith into an isolated part of life. As long as it remains there, all is well. Outside that limited arena, faith ceases to apply.

For too many Christians, this faith functions like a safety deposit box at the bank. We put in it those precious possessions that we want kept secure and that we don't expect to need very often. We always know where these valuables are, but we don't have to bother with them except in special emergencies.

Kangaroo Faith

Our faith becomes a separate little part of our lives. We tuck the private affairs of life into it like a kangaroo's pouch. With our valuables inside the convenient compartment, we can jump from one area of business to another without their getting in the way. We feel better knowing that our convictions are safely out of the way, but within easy reach just in case we need them.

A nationally known Christian businessman provided evidence of the "great divorce" in the business world when he told an interviewer, "I speak of faith in my company as if it were a religion. I believe in God, family, and my restaurant—and in the office that order is reversed."

Students of religious history have a term for this whole phenomenon. They call it "secularization," the process through which ever growing segments of society are freed from the influence of religious faith and institutions. Os Guiness calls this "the Cheshire-Cat factor: because once the process is complete, all that is left of the church is a benign smile like that of the cat in Lewis Carroll's famous tale" *(The Gravedigger File, IVP, 1983).*

Only the scope of the problem is new. For centuries, Christians have wrestled with the relationship of the sacred and the secular. At times, only those obviously religious concerns of life were said to be important to the true saint. Everything except prayer, Bible study, worship, and a few other areas belonged to the world. The real Christians only tolerated these secular concerns so they could devote the rest of their lives to God. During the Middle Ages, even monks were designated as "sacred" or "secular," depending on the degree of preoccupation with religious as opposed to worldly affairs.

The First-century Divorce Experts

The Pharisees of Jesus day knew nothing of what we call "secularization," but they were experts at the great divorce. They divided faith and life with a surgeon's skill. Their scalpels were legalism and ritualism. With their legalistic rule-keeping, they devised a system whereby certain rules were more important than others. These all-important rules became more sacred than the lesser rules. Any areas of life not covered by the rules were free from the constraints of religion.

Ritualism, or the preoccupation with religious ceremony, occupied the highest order of sacred responsibility for the Pharisees. Sabbath keeping, ritual washings, and other prescribed observances became the essentials. Lesser issues of day-to-day life were not nearly as important.

Jesus' last three illustrations of extraordinary righteousness exposed the difference between a life lived totally under the rule of God and one in which God's control is limited to a few sacred closets. In the first three examples, Jesus focused on the inner roots of righteousness and sin. In these final three, He looked at the outer or social results of kingdom living. In each case, He revealed the fruit that grows from the life ruled by God.

Honest to God

The fourth illustration of kingdom conduct reflects an ancient practice much different from that familiar to the modern reader. The taking of oaths or vows was a common part of Jewish life. Technically, an oath was an appeal to God to witness to the truth of a claim or promise. To make an oath was to insist that one's words were more than just idle chatter. An oath brought God into the conversation. He was the guarantor of the truth.

The Old Testament background for the practice of oath-taking came from several different texts. Exodus 20:7 said, "You shall not misuse the name of the Lord your God, for the Lord will not hold anyone guiltless who misuses his name." To appeal to God was a serious matter. One was not to approach the divine name lightly.

Leviticus 19:12 linked the third commandment and oath-taking. "Do not swear falsely by my name and so profane the name of your God. I am the Lord." Faithfulness in keeping an oath was the rule. "When a man makes a vow to the Lord or takes an oath to obligate himself by a pledge, he must not break his word but must do everything he said" (Numbers 30:2). The motive for such oath-keeping was respect for God. "Fear the Lord your God and serve him. Hold fast to him and take your oaths in his name" (Deuteronomy 10:20).

The fact that such laws about oath-taking existed acknowledged that lying also existed. If everyone always told the truth and did everything that was promised, oaths would have been unnecessary. The regulations also sought to limit oaths to only the most serious matters.

An Exception for Every Rule

By the time of Jesus, the rabbis had developed a detailed system of oath-taking and keeping. As with the rest of the Old Covenant, they multiplied the rules and then invented exceptions. An entire section of the Mishnah, the oral traditions of the rabbis, was devoted to this subject.

One reason that oaths became so important an issue was that they provided the basis for what modern lawyers term "contract law." Today, law books spell out in detail the terms and conditions under which an agreement is binding on individuals or business. The law covers everything, including who makes offers, how certain kinds of offers may be accepted or rejected, and the circumstances under which an otherwise valid agreement can be nullified. For example, most state laws consider verbal agreements binding except when certain amounts of money are involved or when the time involved exceeds a set period.

Jewish law had little of this. Instead, it had the regulations concerning oaths. Like contract law, the oath laws made certain agreements binding, but allowed others to be broken unless a predetermined formula was used. All of this was designed to insure honesty. Unfortunately, a dishonest man can always find a new way to cheat his neighbor no matter what safeguards the law prescribes. A dishonest lawyer can even cheat someone by hiding behind the details of the law.

This was exactly what Jesus accused the Pharisees of doing. They not only knew the law; they also knew how to use the law to further their own selfish interests. Listen to His scathing rebuke of their legalized lying:

> Woe to you, blind guides! You say, "If anyone swears by the temple, it means nothing; but if anyone swears by the gold of the temple, he is bound by his oath." You blind fools! Which is greater: the gold, or the temple that makes the gold sacred? You also say, "If anyone swears by the altar, it means nothing; but if anyone swears by the gift on it, he is bound by his oath." You blind men! Which is greater: the gift, or the altar that makes the gift sacred? Therefore, he who swears by the altar swears by it and by everything on it. And he who swears by the temple swears by it and by the one who dwells in it. And he who swears by heaven swears by God's throne and by the one who sits on it (Matthew 23:16-22).

Their practice was clear. Certain promises had to be kept. Others didn't.

Nothing but the Truth

Jesus offered a radical solution. The Old Testament and the rabbis sought to insure honesty by establishing oaths. If God's name was called upon, then the truth was guaranteed. The theory seemed valid enough. But Jesus went deeper. "Do not swear at all," He insisted.

Jesus called upon His disciples to recognize that God was the witness of every word and deed. They didn't have to call upon His name. He was already there. Every word and promise they spoke was done in His presence. No area of life could be viewed as off-limits from God. Heaven, earth, the holy city, even life itself were all under the sovereign control of God. All promises, not just religious oaths, were sacred.

How literally are we to take Jesus words? That is a question that Christians have debated for centuries. Some have contended that this passage rules out any and all forms of oaths, even in a courtroom. If this was what Jesus meant, neither He nor Paul practiced what He taught. Jesus answered the high priest's question under oath without raising an objection (Matthew 26:63, 64). Paul frequently called upon the Lord to witness his words and actions (Romans 1:9; 2 Corinthians 1:23; Galatians 1:20; Philippians 1:8; 1 Thessalonians 2:5, 10; 5:27). The writer of Hebrews even cites God's oath-taking as evidence of His trustworthiness (Hebrews 6:17).

Jesus calls for honesty that goes beyond oath-taking. His disciples' word must be their bond. Simply to forbid oaths lessens the demands.

How does this apply to the everyday life of today's disciple? First, there are no double standards. The same principles of integrity apply to business as to religious activities. Second, all forms of legal dishonesty are forbidden. Even if the law says that an agreement isn't valid until the contract is signed, the disciple's word is enough. Next, lying of every sort is eliminated. Stretching and withholding the truth are as much lies as outright fabrications.

Jesus' words also spotlight the power of the tongue. A dishonest heart is first revealed by a dishonest mouth. Truthful speech generally leads the way for truthful living. Finally, a proper understanding of this issue casts a new light on profanity. If all of life is sacred and lived out in the presence of God, then to speak lightly of God or any part of His creation is a sacrilege. Profanity dishonors God by making everything common.

Going the Second Mile—and Beyond

No Old Testament law is more misunderstood than the one Jesus cited next. "An eye for an eye and a tooth for a tooth" is often quoted as a proverb encouraging revenge and retaliation. Nothing could be further from the law's original intention.

These words are found in three different contexts in the Old Testament (Exodus 21:24, 25; Leviticus 24:19, 20; Deuteronomy

19:15-21). In each, the law was a part of the formal legal system of Israel, not the individual's response to mistreatment. The law actually limited revenge. "A tooth for a tooth" meant that a punishment should fit the crime. Just because someone knocked out my tooth, I would not be entitled to demand his life.

The Old Testament denounced personal revenge in the clearest terms. "Do not seek revenge or bear a grudge against one of your people, but love your neighbor as yourself. I am the Lord" (Leviticus 19:18). Soloman taught, "Do not say, 'I'll pay you back for this wrong!' Wait for the Lord, and he will deliver you" (Proverbs 20:22). "Do not say, 'I'll do to him as he has done to me; I'll pay that man back for what he did'" (Proverbs 24:29).

By the first century, a system of financial compensations had replaced the literal "eye for an eye." If a man caused injury to a neighbor's tooth or eye, he was required to pay a set fee. Such modifications were still within the scope and intent of the law.

As with the other examples cited by Jesus, the Pharisees ripped the original law from its context, turning it into an excuse to do exactly what God had forbidden. On one hand, an "eye for an eye" became an excuse for personal vendettas. On the other, it was a legal right to be exercised at the slightest provocation.

Waiting for God's Justice

Jesus returned the law to its original setting and pointed to its deeper purpose. He called for His disciples to eliminate, not just limit, revenge. He advocated a radical indifference to personal attacks and injuries. Instead of turning against the one who had caused harm, Jesus called for turning the matter over to God.

Jesus cited four real-life examples of this principle. Each one came from first-century society. The first, a blow to the right cheek, was more of a personal insult than an actual physical attack. The proper response was to turn the other cheek and accept the humiliation rather than to reply in kind. The second covered one's legal rights. Under Jewish law, a man could be sued for his coat, the inner garment, but no one could take his cloak or outer garment. Jesus told His disciples to forgo even this basic right.

The third illustration, being forced to go a mile, involved political oppression. Under Roman law, a citizen could be conscripted to carry a soldier's or imperial messenger's baggage for a thousand paces. Jesus told His disciples to volunteer to go a second thousand. The final illustrations involved the beggar and the borrower. Give, don't resist, was the rule of conduct.

Each situation involved an invasion of the disciple's personal life. One's pride, legal rights, privacy, and possessions were no longer to be the number-one concern of life. Instead, each of these areas were to be surrendered to God. If vengeance or punishment were to be executed, God was to do it.

Paul appealed to this same principle:

> Do not repay anyone evil for evil. Be careful to do what is right in the eyes of everybody. If it is possible, as far as it depends on you, live at peace with everyone. Do not take revenge, my friends, but leave room for God's wrath (Romans 12:17-19).

Paul was convinced that God's rule extended to every problem and adversity of life. His purpose was bigger than any personal problem a Christian might face. If that were the case, the Christian could resist the temptation to get even with his adversary. He knew he had a defender who would always do what was right. He didn't have to look out for himself because that was God's job.

Attitudes and Actions

Again we face the same issue that we have confronted with Jesus' other examples of kingdom righteousness. How literally are we to take these instructions? Some have suggested that they must be obeyed to the letter. Evil must not be resisted at all. Tolstoy advocated the abolition of police and armies because of these words. Others have cited these verses as the basis for pacifism.

One thing should be clear by now. Simply to take Jesus' teachings literally often misses the very principle He was teaching. For example, did Jesus mean that His disciples should willingly go the second mile when forced to carry a soldier's pack, but dig in their heels and refuse to go one step further when that second mile was completed. Jesus' concern included the attitude as well as the action. Even literally, turning the other cheek was not enough. Augustine was right when he observed, "Many have learned how to offer the other cheek, but do not know how to love him by whom they were struck."

Jesus and Paul both stood their ground when they were personally attacked (John 18:22, 23; Acts 16:37). Furthermore, Jesus' instructions about church discipline and resolving personal differences assumes that there is a time and place to demand justice (Matthew 18:15-17). Paul didn't take Jesus literally when he told one church no longer to give to asking brothers who refused to work (2 Thessalonians 3:10).

Turning the other cheek and going the second mile require an attitude of love and self denial. Above all, they require an absolute dependence on God. Giving to whoever asks means realizing that I no longer possess anything. All belongs to God. I am free to give because I have been relieved of any duty to preserve and protect. God takes care of what is His, including me.

Like Father, Like Son

Jesus' final illustration brings the section to a fitting climax. God's rule includes not only every business dealing and every personal problem of the disciple's life; it also covers every person. No one can draw a circle and limit his faith to his relationship with those on the inside. The disciple's love, like God's love, extends to all.

Love was the central precept of the Old Testament. Jesus and the Pharisees knew that (Matthew 22:34-40). Nowhere was hatred encouraged. In fact, the law required that the same compassion be shown to an enemy as would be shown to a neighbor (Exodus 23:4, 5). It was the Old Testament, and not just the New Testament, that taught that one should feed and clothe his enemy (Proverbs 25:21, 22; Romans 12:20).

As far as we know, none of the rabbis went so far as to teach that the law said a person was to hate his enemies. Others did however. The Jewish zealots, the anti-Roman political group, advocated hatred and bloodshed against all Romans and any Jews who conspired with them. The Dead Sea Scrolls reveal that the strict Jewish sects who secluded themselves in their own private communities in the wilderness required their members to pledge their loyalty to the group and their hatred for outsiders.

While the Pharisees and the scribes may not have taught outright hatred, they did limit their love. Anyone who was not just like them or who failed to live up to their standards of conduct frequently became objects of contempt. The Samaritans, especially, were outside the Jewish circle of love.

The Jewish-Samaritan hatred evolved from centuries of religious and civil strife. By the time of Jesus, the animosity had reached unbelievable dimensions. Early in the first century, some Samaritans had desecrated the temple by scattering human bones throughout the sanctuary at night. The Jews refused to eat food prepared by a Samaritan. Anything touched by a Samaritan was declared unclean. A whole village might be pronounced unclean if a Samaritan woman entered the town. Jewish pilgrims normally would travel far out of their way rather than set foot on Samaritan soil when traveling between Galilee and Judea.

Against this background, Jesus' parable of the Good Samaritan must have startled his Jewish hearers (Luke 10:25-37). He didn't tell a story about a Jew who helped an injured Samaritan. That would have been bad enough. He made the Samaritan the hero! The Samaritan stopped to do what a priest and Levite had refused to do for a fellow Jew.

The Limits of Love

This parable aptly illustrates the principles Jesus was teaching in a call for God-like love. The disciple's love must be as all-encompassing as the Heavenly Father's. If God's rule includes all of life, then His love must include all people.

Jesus taught that the responsibility to act lovingly toward another is not determined by any of the following:

Who the other person is. The Samaritan didn't stop to check the injured man's birth certificate. He was hurt and needed help. That was all that mattered.

I must love the poor and the rich, the Samaritan and the Jew. I should pray for and help my adversary as well as my neighbor.

How the person treats me. No doubt, the Samaritan had been mistreated by many Jews in his lifetime. At the very least, he had heard horror stories about the dealings between his countrymen and the Jews. But none of that mattered. Genuine love forgets everything but how to help.

My reaction is not determined by the others' actions. I am ruled by a higher order. Even if he curses, I bless. He may attack me, but I still will love.

How much it costs me. The Samaritan risked his own safety and spent his own money to help his Jewish neighbor. He even signed a "blank check," promising to pay any future bills. No one promised to pay him back.

Real love is costly. It always leads to sacrifice. No one knew that better than Jesus. Love never keeps score or calculates the potential profit or loss. It only sees a need and the opportunity to meet it.

Jesus cites the only model for such love—God himself. In His day-to-day blessings on His creation, and especially on the cross, God demonstrated a love for the very ones who were His self-proclaimed enemies (Romans 5:6-11). Jesus literally prayed for His persecutors and gave His life for those who wanted to take it from Him.

Blessed Are the Peacemakers

Peter had witnessed this divine love. He knew Jesus practiced what He preached and expected His disciples to do the same. "To this you were called," Peter wrote,

> because Christ suffered for you, leaving you an example, that you should follow in his steps
> "He committed no sin,
> and no deceit was found in his mouth."
> When they hurled their insults at him, he did not retaliate; when he suffered, he made no threats. Instead, he entrusted himself to him who judges justly. He himself bore our sins in his body on the tree, so that we might die to sins and live for righteousness; by his wounds you have been healed (1 Peter 2:21-24).

Such love is truly extraordinary. The world knows little about it. The law of the world is love those who love you. The law of the kingdom is much simpler: love, period!

Loving an enemy is much harder than signing a peace treaty. But in the long haul, only love can make for lasting peace. This is why the peacemakers and those who love their enemies are both called the "sons of God" (Matthew 5:9, 45). God is the author of peace and love. All His children follow in His footsteps.

Here lies the reason the child of God loves even his enemies—he is a child of God. It is a matter of "heredity," not environment.

The Perfect Christian

Jesus ended His call for kingdom righteousness where He began. He demanded something more than the commonplace. Living and loving like the unbelievers will never do. Even matching the most religious Pharisees rule for rule isn't enough. Jesus calls for extraordinary righteousness and extraordinary love.

"Be perfect, therefore, as your heavenly Father is perfect" (Matthew 5:48) is a call to abandon all standards except one. The Old Testament said the same thing, "Be holy because I, the Lord your God, am holy" (Leviticus 19:2). The Greek text of the law even used the same term for *perfect* when it declared, "you must be *blameless* before the Lord your God" (Deuteronomy 18:13). The same is used to contrast Solomon and David. "As Solomon grew old, his wives turned his heart after other gods, and his heart was not fully *devoted* to the Lord his God, as the heart of David his father had been" (1 Kings 11:4).

God-like perfection does not always mean sinlessness. It does mean to be pure in heart. It means hungering and thirsting for a righteousness that is found only in God. It means being totally and completely submitted to the rule of God. It seeks first the kingdom of God and His righteousness.

Chapter Eight

How to Be Religious
Without Being a Christian
Matthew 6:1-8

At Matthew 6, Jesus led His followers to a major intersection on the straight and narrow. The journey began with a portrait of the disciple's inner character (Matthew 5:1-12) and his outer influence in the world (Matthew 5:13-15). Following this introduction, Jesus erected the first signpost for the initial leg of the journey (Matthew 5:17-20). He called for extraordinary righteousness that went above and beyond the call of duty. In six startling illustrations, Jesus contrasted the external rules of the scribes and Pharisees with the inner rule of God that was to control the heart of the disciple (Matthew 5:21-48).

Throughout these teachings, Jesus contrasted the citizens of the kingdom with three different groups: the scribes, the Pharisees, and the Gentiles or pagans. Thus far, he focused mainly on the traditions of the scribes or the religious lawyers. In the final illustration, He introduced the self-oriented love of the pagans (Matthew 5:46-48). He here turned His attention to the religion of the Pharisees.

Actually the scribes and the Pharisees were very closely associated. The scribes were the theological experts while the Pharisees were the faithful "laymen" who tried to practice what the scribes taught. Neither group would have been offended by the fact that Jesus lumped them together.

But the pagans? That was another matter! Jesus dared to tar the scribes, the Pharisees, and the Gentiles with the same brush. All three stood alienated from God. He warned His disciples that life in the kingdom must be lived by a different pattern from any of these groups.

Here Jesus turned His attention away from the ethical and moral conduct of those in the kingdom and to what normally might be considered religious activities. He terms them "acts of righteousness." This was a common phrase used to describe a person's duty to God.

Double Love

By including these acts (alms-giving, prayer, and fasting), Jesus acknowledged that the rule of God is not just a matter of private morality. The kingdom involves one's relationship to God as well as to man. Jesus' New Covenant included both the horizontal and vertical relationships just as the Old Covenant had. The Ten Commandments said both, "You shall not murder," and, "You shall not misuse the name of the Lord your God." Both were equally valid. Likewise, Jesus insisted that the disciple who lives under the rule of God must both pray and love his enemy. Both responsibilities belong to the kingdom.

This dual emphasis is important. It keeps us from making Jesus into something less than He really was. He was not just an ethical teacher who was determined to show men how to live more peacefully and happily with one another. He wasn't just a moral philosopher who pointed men to the true route to inner tranquility.

He was God's Messiah—*and* the world's savior! He came to point *men* to *God*. His task was to reconcile men to one another by first reconciling them to their Creator.

Jesus knew nothing of religion-less Christianity that measures discipleship solely in terms of political or social activism. Following Jesus requires more than living by the Golden Rule. The first standard of the kingdom was not brother-love. It was God-love! Out of this divine relationship flowed the power and the purpose that made radical human love possible.

In the Sermon on the Mount, Jesus insisted that the life ruled by God is personal *and* social; ethical *and* theological; private *and* public. In short, the life of a disciple is a total life lived in total submission to God.

The three areas Jesus included in the religious life of the kingdom are not necessarily the only ones. He might have included other items such as praise and worship or study of the Scriptures. But He included the three areas that were held most sacred to the Jewish faithful and to most other religions as well. These three duties also cover the spectrum of human relationships. Alms-giving involves one's attitude and response to other people. Prayer focuses on God. Fasting centers on the discipline of the self.

84

Jesus assumed that these activities were right and proper. But He also assumed that not everyone who did them did so in a right and proper manner. One can do a right thing in a wrong way. One can be religious without being a Christian! In this chapter, we will examine how Jesus applied this principle to giving. The next two chapters will focus on prayer and fasting.

Lending to God

First, consider the similarities between the practices of the Pharisees and the teachings of Jesus. Both insisted that men ought to give to the poor. The term translated as "alms" or "giving to the needy" literally meant "acts of mercy." As students of the Old Testament, the Pharisees knew that God placed a high priority on concern for the poor and disadvantaged. Since He was a God of mercy, He expected His people to do likewise.

Under the law, compassion was to take precedence over profit! The Jews were to leave part of the grain or groves for the poor to glean (Leviticus 19:9, 10; Deuteronomy 24:20, 21). Widows and orphans were to be given a place in the religious feasts (Deuteronomy 16:11, 14). Poverty was not to prevent one from joining in the celebration of God's worship and bounty. Also, the Old Testament designated a part of the tithe for the care of the widows and orphans (Deuteronomy 26:12-13). Deuteronomy 15:7, 8 summarizes the sentiments of the entire law:

> If there is a poor man among your brothers in any of the towns of the land that the Lord your God is giving you, do not be hardhearted or tightfisted toward your poor brother. Rather be openhanded and freely lend him whatever he needs.

Solomon taught that a generous man would be blessed (Proverbs 22:9). One who oppressed the poor would face the judgment of God (Proverbs 22:22, 23). On the other hand, a man who was kind to the poor was lending to God. He would repay (Proverbs 19:17). The prophets frequently warned against taking advantage of the poor and oppressed. (See Isaiah 1:17; Amos 2:6, 7.)

The rabbis took this concern one step further. At least some of them taught that alms-giving atoned for sin (Tobit 12:9). Even though they distorted the Old Testament emphasis, they rightly maintained the importance of showing practical compassion and concern for the needy.

The New Testament continued this same priority. Jesus taught that whether one fed the hungry, clothed the naked, and cared for the needs of oppressed and disadvantaged brothers would be a factor in the final judgment (Matthew 25:31-46). Such concern was a "religious" duty, not just a social obligation according to Jesus. "Whatever you did for one of the least of these brothers of mine, you did for me," He insisted (Matthew 25:40).

The Witness of Love

The early church practiced radical concern for the poor. Anyone who had more than enough gave of what he had so that no one went without. The Christians sold goods and property so that hungry brothers and sisters could be fed (Acts 2:45; 4:34-36). The result was that "there were no needy persons among them" (Acts 4:34). This unparalleled demonstration of love no doubt had much to do with the rapid spread of the gospel (Acts 2:47). Concern for the poor and hungry continued into the next generation and crossed national and cultural boundaries as Greek and Gentile believers sacrificed to help their Jewish Christian brothers in their time of need (1 Corinthians 16:1, 2; 2 Corinthians 8—9).

James termed such giving a mark of true religion (James 1:27) and the proof of genuine faith (James 2:14-19). John called it the evidence of Christlike love.

> If anyone has material possessions and sees his brother in need but has no pity on him, how can the love of God be in him? Dear children, let us not love with words or tongue but with actions and in truth. This then is how we know that we belong to the truth, and how we set our hearts at rest in his presence whenever our hearts condemn us. For God is greater than our hearts, and he knows everything (1 John 3:17-20).

A History of Love

This demonstration of practical concern for the poor and disadvantaged continued during the early centuries of the faith. Adolph Harnack, in his classic work *The Mission and Expansion of Christianity in the First Three Centuries,* insists that such demonstrations of love were a major reason for the powerful witness of the early Christians. In a chapter entitled "The Gospel of Love and Charity," he lists several ways that these Christians put their faith in practice. According to Harnack, they cared for widows and orphans, the sick, prisoners, and slaves. They also ministered to people who had suffered disasters, those without jobs, and fellow Christians who were traveling and needed a place to stay.

Many testimonies to early Christian charity can be found in the literature of the centuries that followed the birth of the church. Aristides, a second-century Greek philosopher, described the Christians in an address to the Roman Emperor Hadrian:

> They love one another; and from the widows they do not turn away their countenance; and they rescue the orphan from him who does him violence; and he who has gives to him who has not, without grudging. . . . When one of the poor passes away from the world, and any of them sees him, then he provides for his burial according to his ability; and if they hear that any of their number is imprisoned or oppressed for the name of their Messiah, all of them provide for his needs, and if it is possible that he may be delivered, they deliver him. If there is among them a man that is poor or needy, and they have not an abundance of necessities, they fast two or three days that they may supply the needy with their necessary food.

Tertullian, an early third-century Christian writer and scholar wrote, "It is our care for the helpless, our practice of loving kindness, that brands us in the eyes of many of our opponents. 'Only look,' they say, 'look how they love one another.'" He explained how the Christians cared for the needs of the poor from their voluntary contributions.

> Each of us puts in a small amount one day a month, or whenever he pleases; but only if he pleases and if he is able, for there is no compulsion in the matter, everyone contributing of his own free will. These monies are, as it were, the deposits of piety. They are expended upon no banquets or drinking-bouts or thankless eating-houses, but on feeding and burying poor people, on behalf of boys and girls who have neither parents nor money, in support of old folk unable now to go about, as well as for people who are shipwrecked, or who may be in the mines or exiled in islands or in prison—so long as their distress is for the sake of God's fellowship—themselves the nurslings of their confession.

Julian the Apostate, an arch-enemy of the early church, offered this backhanded critique of the early Christians. "These godless

Galileans," he complained, "feed not only their own poor but ours; our poor lack our care." Lucian, another non-Christian wrote that the Christians "become incredibly alert when anything of this kind occurs, that affects their common interests. On such occasions no expense is grudged."

The Christians explained that their extraordinary love was due to their extraordinary Lord. Justin Martyr (AD 165) wrote,

> We used to value above all else money and possessions; now we bring together all that we have and share it with those who are in need [cf. Acts 4:34-37]. Formerly, we hated and killed one another and, because of a difference in nationality or custom, we refused to admit strangers within our gates. Now since the coming of Christ, we all live in peace. We pray for our enemies and seek to convert those who hate us unjustly. . . .

It is true that there have been times when those who claimed to follow Christ were just as selfish and thoughtless as the rest of humanity. But more often than not, those who were most faithful to Jesus and His kingdom were also the most concerned about meeting the needs of the poor and oppressed.

The Old Testament, the Pharisees, Jesus, and the early Christians all taught the importance of giving to the poor as a demonstration of one's genuine relationship with God. But Jesus insisted that the righteous acts of His kingdom people differed from the practices of the Pharisees at three important points.

A Villain With a Smiling Cheek

The Pharisees gave, prayed, and fasted to be seen and honored by men (Matthew 6:1, 2, 5). While there may have been many devout and honest Pharisees, Jesus was convinced that there were also many who served God from less than the best motives. He called them "hypocrites," a term that came from the Greek theater. It described a play actor or a pretender. While the term may not have had all the negative connotations then as it does now, it was certainly no compliment. Jesus made this clear when He told the Pharisees,

> You hypocrites! You are like whitewashed tombs, which look beautiful on the outside but on the inside are full of dead men's bones and everything unclean. In the same way, on the outside you appear to

people as righteous but on the inside you are full of hypocrisy and wickedness" (Matthew 23:27, 28).

Shakespeare echoed this portrait of perverted religion when he wrote,

The devil can cite Scripture for his purpose.
An evil soul, producing holy witness;
Is like a villain with a smiling cheek;
a goodly apple rotten at the heart;
Oh, what a goodly outside falsehood hath!
(Quoted in *Webster's Encyclopedia of Dictionaries,* 1958, p. 884).

The Pharisees worshiped God with their lips, not their hearts, Jesus charged (Matthew 15:7-9). The root of their problem was a concern for appearances. "Everything they do is done for men to see" (Matthew 23:5).

The Overflow of Grace

The disciple's giving was for an entirely different reason. He was to show no concern whatsoever for the applause or appreciation of men. Giving to the poor was the natural result of a desire to meet a need and glorify God in the process. Knowing that God knew was enough.

Paul echoed this same motive when he spoke of the generosity of his fellow Christians in a time of need. Writing to the Corinthians, he said,

This service that you perform is not only supplying the needs of God's people but is also overflowing in many expressions of thanks to God. Because of the service by which you have proved yourselves, men will praise God for the obedience that accompanies your confession of the gospel of Christ, and for your generosity in sharing with them and with everyone else (2 Corinthians 9:12, 13).

Is the promise of a reward a motive for the disciple's giving? Jesus certainly stresses the place of the reward. "Then your Father, who sees what is done in secret, will reward you" (Matthew 6:4). Jesus, however, seems to rule out the kind of calculated giving that first examines the worth of the reward before deciding whether to make the sacrifice or not.

89

Self-forgetful Giving

The fact that reward had little to do with the motive for helping those in need is clear from Jesus' directions on alms-giving and the picture of the final judgment He provided in Matthew 25. "Do not let your left hand know what your right hand is doing," He told them (Matthew 6:3). Taken literally, such a command is absurd. Short of amputation, how can one part of the body be kept ignorant of what another part does? It can't! Jesus' point, however, is not literal. He calls for giving that is devoid of any self-centeredness. The giver gives neither to receive the applause of men or of self. He wears blinders. All he sees is the need he can help meet. Even a reward from God would be the last thing on such a disciple's mind at the moment of the sharing.

Such self-forgetfulness marked the righteous in Jesus' parable of the sheep and the goats (Matthew 25:31-46). When told of the reward they would receive because they had ministered to Jesus, those on the right expressed surprise. "Lord, when did we see you hungry and feed you, or thirsty and give you something to drink?" they asked (Matthew 25:37). Their service had been given totally without regard for anything but the need of the moment. It had never occurred to them that "giving to the least of these" could result in a divine reward.

To Shine or to Hide

The Pharisees' motive, to be seen of men, affected the manner of their alms-giving. Jesus portrays them in a very picturesque fashion. They announced their acts with trumpets in the synagogues and on the streets, He said. Whether this was literal or an exaggeration for effect, the point is clear. They gave in such a way as to maximize the attention and acclaim they received. The disciple, on the other hand, was to give secretly and selflessly. Only the all-seeing Father was to observe their deeds.

These instructions create a problem. How can the disciple let his "light shine before men, that they may see [his] good deeds and praise your Father in heaven" (Matthew 5:16) and keep his acts of righteousness a secret at the same time? At least part of the tension evaporates when the two passages are returned to their contexts. The good deeds that men see are probably better understood as the fruit of the qualities outlined in the Beatitudes. Humility, meekness, mercy, and the like are the moral foundations that lead to the kind of life Jesus outlined in His six illustrations of exceeding righteousness (Matthew 5:21-48). These moral fruits are to abound for all to see.

The "acts of righteousness," on the other hand, are private expressions of the disciple's relationship with God. They may be seen by others, but they are not to be done for *the purpose* of being seen.

Jesus' two statements actually addressed two different sets of problems. The call to secret giving was an antidote to hypocrisy. The admonition to public good deeds, on the other hand, called for courageous faith in the face of persecution. A. B. Bruce summarized both of the Lord's instructions in the memorable words, "Shine where tempted to hide; hide where tempted to shine." Both actions were for the same purpose—to glorify God.

Paid in Full

The hypocrite who gave to be seen received exactly what he wanted and nothing more. "They have received their reward in full," Jesus said. The phrase *in full* was a term from the commercial world of the day. It described an account that was paid in full and closed. Nothing more was due.

The disciple gave secretly to meet the needs of the poor. No one saw but God. But God sees, He remembers, and He rewards. What is the reward that the Father bestows on His children? Certainly Heaven and the inheritance in the kingdom is part of it (Matthew 25:34). It also includes increased opportunity for service (Matthew 25:21). The joy of seeing God honored and pleased must be at the center of the disciple's reward. "Come and share your master's happiness" was the blessing given the faithful servant (Matthew 25:21, 23).

Jesus outlined the true treasure of the faithful disciple in the seven blessings with which He began the constitution of the kingdom:

> theirs is the kingdom of heaven,
> they will be comforted,
> they will inherit the earth,
> they will be filled,
> they will be shown mercy,
> they will see God, and
> they will be called the sons of God.

Those with their eyes set on the world and the applause of men will find little worth wanting here. But for the one who loves God and whose desire more than anything else is to know Him, this is treasure beyond compare. Nothing could be greater!

Whatever the reward, Jesus made one thing clear. It is all because of grace. Nothing the disciple does could merit the blessings of the kingdom (cf. Matthew 20: 1-16). As Paul reminded his readers,

> For it is by grace you have been saved, through faith—and this not from yourselves, it is the gift of God—not by works, so that no one can boast. For we are God's workmanship, created in Christ Jesus to do good works, which God prepared in advance for us to do (Ephesians 2:8-10).

The Last Pharisee

Jesus contrasted two totally different religious systems. They each had different motives, manners, and rewards. But the biggest difference was in their view of God.

One religious system talked about God; the other talked to Him personally and intimately. One knew about Him; the other knew Him as Father. One knew God in the past tense; the other worshiped Him as present reality.

The last Pharisee has long since vanished from the earth. But he left behind many heirs. Wherever men turn religion into a performance rather than a personal relationship with the living God, Pharisees are alive and well.

Chapter Nine

Prayer's Counterfeit
Matthew 6:8-15

According to Jesus, not all prayer is really prayer. Like charity, prayer can sometimes become nothing more than a religious act. When that happens, the words, no matter how pious and proper, are not prayer. Counterfeit prayer requires only a cast of one. The real thing involves man *and* God.

Richard Crashaw describes the difference:

> Two went to pray? Oh, rather say
> One went to brag, the other to pray;
> One stands up close and treads on high
> Where the other dares not send his eye;
> One near to God's altar trod,
> The other to the altar's God.
> (Quoted in the *Encyclopedia of Religious Quotations,* Revell, 1965, p. 339).

The Facts of Prayer

To understand Jesus' alternative to counterfeit prayer, one must understand a few basic facts about prayer.

First, prayer is a promise of God. It is not a human invention or a formula brewed in a witchdoctor's cauldron to secure the favor of the gods. It is a gift of God. "The Lord is near to all who call on him, to all who call on him in truth," wrote David. "He fulfills the desires of those who fear him; he hears their cry and saves them" (Psalm 145:18, 19). According to Solomon, "The prayer of the upright pleases him" (Proverbs 15:8).

Jesus extended the promise of prayer. "If you believe, you will receive whatever you ask for in prayer," He told His disciples (Matthew 21:22). He taught that answering prayer was a natural thing for God, just as natural as a father's meeting the needs of his child (Matthew 7:9-11; Luke 11:13). "My Father will give you whatever you ask in my name" (John 16:23).

But while it is a promise, real prayer is not without limits. It is, in fact, a privilege reserved for those who are on speaking terms with God. Faith (Hebrews 11:6), certainty (James 1:5, 6), humility (James 4:10), and righteousness (James 5:16) are all prerequisites of effective prayer. Jeremiah cited the most important ingredient when he wrote, "You will call upon me and come and pray to me, and I will listen to you. You will seek me and find me when you seek me with all your heart" (Jeremiah 29:12, 13).

R. A. Torrey tells of a lady who attended his church, but who had never accepted the Lord. One day, she exclaimed to Dr. Torrey, "I don't believe in the Bible!"

"Why is that," he asked.

"I have tried its promises and they are not true."

"Which ones are not true," Torrey countered.

"The one that says 'Whatever ye desire in prayer, ye shall receive.' I have tried that promise and it has failed. Tell me, if I have not received what I desired, hasn't it failed?" she demanded.

"Not at all," insisted the preacher.

"Isn't that what the Bible says?"

"Yes," replied Torrey, "It does say something to that effect."

"Then how can you say it hasn't failed?"

"First," he said, "You need to ask if you are one of the 'ye.'"

Real prayer is a privilege reserved for the child of God. But it is one that extends to every child of God, not to just a select few. In the marvelous book, *The Kneeling Christian,* the author says,

> Of all the millions in India living in the bondage of Hinduism, none may pray except the Brahmins! A millionaire merchant of any other caste must get a Brahmin—often a mere boy at school—to say his prayer for him. The Muslim cannot pray unless he has learned a few phrases of Arabic, for his god hears only prayers offered in what they believe to be the holy language.

Not so with prayer to the living God of the Bible. He hears all His children.

The Problem of Prayer

Even Jesus' disciples found prayer to be a problem. They no doubt knew the prayer-promises of God. As Jews, they were accustomed to praying. But when they watched and listened to Jesus pray, they knew something was missing. They had seen Jesus pray often. At His baptism (Luke 3:21), at His transfiguration (Luke 9:28, 29), and on the night before He chose the Twelve, He had spent many hours in prayer. Later they would be present as He agonized in prayer all through the night before His crucifixion (Matthew 26:36-45).

Their request was a natural one. "Lord, teach us to pray," they asked (Luke 11:1). The disciples didn't ask Jesus to teach them "how" to pray. They wanted Him to help them become men of prayer. They knew how to pray. The problem was that their prayers lacked the fervency and intimacy with which Jesus spoke to the Heavenly Father.

Prayerlessness remains a major problem of the church. Leonard Ravenhill's indictment of the modern church is far too true. In his book *Why Revival Tarries,* he writes,

> Poverty stricken as the church is today in many things, she is most stricken here, in the place of prayer. We have many organizers, but few agonizers; many players and payers, few prayers; many singers, few clingers; lots of pastors, few wrestlers; many fears, few tears; much fashion, little passion; many interferers, few intercessors; many writers, few fighters. Failing here, we fail everywhere (Bethany House Publishers, 1979, p. 23).

No Room for Doubt

Why the problem with prayer? Why do we have such difficulty with real prayer? Sometimes the problem is a matter of faith. We simply don't believe. Real prayer grows from conviction. The man or woman of prayer must believe God is real. "Anyone who comes to [God] must believe that he exists and that he rewards those who earnestly seek him" (Hebrews 11:6). A doubting, uncertain disciple seldom prays.

Praying also assumes that God cares about the needs of those who call upon Him and is that He is willing to act to meet those needs. A person who worships a reluctant God will always be a reluctant prayer. The God of prayer must also be able to act. "Surely the arm of the Lord is not too short to save, nor his ear too dull to hear," the prophet Isaiah reminded ancient Israel (Isaiah 59:1). Prayer makes no sense at all if God is powerless to respond.

But the most basic conviction that is necessary before real prayer can take place is the belief that God has designated prayer as the chief means by which His blessings come to the lives of His people. John Wesley believed this. "God will do nothing," he wrote, "but in answer to prayer." E. M. Bounds declared that "God shapes the world by prayer. . . . The prayers of God's saints are the capital stock of heaven by which God carries on His great work upon earth. God conditions the very life and prosperity of His cause on prayer." No one who fails to believe this can understand the importance and power of believing prayer.

The Hard Work of Praying

A second reason for the frequent problem with prayer experienced by the church is that those who pray give up. Jesus taught His disciples to "pray and not give up" (Luke 18:1). He underscored the lesson with the parable of the persistent widow. The problem is not that it takes the Lord time to decide whether to answer the prayers of His people or not. Often it takes time for us to become serious about our requests.

But the biggest reason that there are so few great prayers in the church is that prayer is hard work. Some contend that prayer is the easy way out. They seem to think that those who pray for God's help are really trying to evade their own responsibilities. Prayer *is* the disciple's responsibility!

And it is far from easy.

Most people find it much less difficult to work than pray. They could do almost anything else for an hour except pray. Praying all night as Jesus did is unthinkable.

His disciples learned this lesson the hard way (Matthew 26:36-45). Jesus asked Peter, James, and John to pray with Him. It was to be their last night with Him. All He asked was that they pray. Instead, they slept. Again He asked them to watch and pray. Again they slept. Peter was ready to fight, but he was not ready to pray.

Praying was harder!

"Watch and pray," Jesus warned them, "so that you will not fall into temptation. The spirit is willing, but the body is weak" (Matthew 26:41). Paul Rader echoed the seriousness of Jesus' call to prayer when he wrote, "If you can beat the devil in the matter of regular daily prayer, you can beat him anywhere. If he can beat you there, he can possibly beat you anywhere."

Prayer: a Disciple's Priority

Because Jesus knew the promise, the privilege, and the problem of prayer, He gave it a place of priority in His ministry to His disciples. He knew that without a life of real, genuine prayer, the life He described in the Sermon on the Mount would never become a reality. A person could live the extraordinary life Jesus described, but not on his own. It requires access to the resources and power of God. Prayer is not an option.

In His description of true righteousness, Jesus contrasts the prayers of the hypocrites and the pagans with real prayer, that expected of the kingdom citizen. The Jews, especially the Pharisees, were praying people. The rabbis taught that a person was to pray five times a day. The faithful Jew prayed upon rising in the morning, before retiring at night, and at three designated hours of prayer during the day (9 AM, noon, and 3 PM). Most Pharisees would go to the synagogue for the hour of prayer. However, if he was otherwise occupied, he would stop wherever he was and recite his prayers.

At morning and night, the rabbis taught that the *Shema* and a special benediction should be recited. These words were based on Israel's belief in the one God and included statements from their most cherished Old Testament Scriptures (Deuteronomy 6:4-9; 11:13-21; Numbers 15:37-41). A special prayer form, known as the Eighteen Benedictions, was used at the other three hours of prayer.

What Prayer Is Not

The problem of the Pharisees was not that they prayed at prescribed times or even that they followed a predetermined prayer formula. Jesus said the problem was their motive. They prayed to be seen of men, not to be heard of God. They received what they wanted and nothing more (Matthew 6:5). The people around witnessed their religion, but God didn't hear their prayers.

Jesus contrasts the difference between real prayer and its counterfeit. Real prayer is not any of these:

A performance. Prayer is not designed to prove to others how religious or spiritual we are. The words used and the occasion chosen ought not be determined by the crowd.

A magic formula. In most pagan religions, prayer is linked with special rituals and incantations designed to manipulate the gods. If the right words were spoken in the right way and in the right place, then the gods had to respond. Even meaningless chatter can affect the gods if continued long enough to overcome their reluctance. The gods become the servant and the one who prays the ruler. "Do not keep on babbling like pagans, for they think they will be heard because of their many words," Jesus admonished His disciples (Matthew 6:7).

Updating God on what's happening. He already knows. If He didn't, He wouldn't be God. "Your Father knows what you need before you ask him," Jesus said (Matthew 6:8). This fact, more than anything else, completely alters the concept of prayer held by many in and out of the church.

What Prayer Is

What is real prayer if it is not performance, a magic formula, or a divine update? Jesus teaches what genuine prayer is.

A private audience with the Creator. "Go into your room, close the door and pray to your Father, who is unseen," Jesus said (Matthew 6:6). The word for *room* was a term used to designate an inner room or closet. The emphasis of prayer is on the personal presence of God, not on the public spectacle or the formal ritual. It is who the disciple is talking to that matters most. If God is truly there, nothing else matters.

Personal communication with the Heavenly Father. The content of prayer flows from the heart. Real prayer can never simply be repeating lines like an actor. Written and prescribed prayer may have their place, but only as a genuine reflection of the mind and soul of the one who prays them.

A product of the disciple's most personal priorities. How a person prays and what he petitions God for reveals what lies closest to his heart. The hypocrite cared most about his religious reputation. His prayers echoed the desires of his heart.

Prayer involves asking, but it is always more than that. Prayer is first adoration of the God in whose presence the believer stands. It is God's desires, not the desires of the one praying, that come first. It can be no other way for the person who recognizes that he is in the presence of the Holy God, who already knows his needs and sees the very thoughts and intents of his heart.

Prayer as a Relationship

This personal view of prayer, which sees it first as a relationship with God, helps explain why the disciple prays even though God already knows his needs. He prays because God has told him to. It is a matter of obedience, not just a way to get what he wants. Prayer also strengthens and builds the personal relationship between the Father in Heaven and the earth-bound child. The poets say that "absence makes the heart grow fonder." Frequent, heartfelt communication does an even better job of growing love. A caring child does not call home only when he wants to ask for something. Speaking with the Father is a natural response of love.

Martin Lloyd-Jones is right when he observes, "Ultimately, therefore, a man discovers the real condition of his spiritual life when he examines himself in prayer, when he is alone with God."

Prayer also builds faith. The more a person talks to God, the more he believes in God. This fact helps explain why persistent prayer is so important. Often God knows the problem of his child and is ready to provide the answer, but He knows that the child is not ready to receive. The answer might create new and bigger problems or responsibilities. It might even stifle the growth of the believer's faith. A quickly answered prayer can easily be discounted as coincidence. But one who prays faithfully and persistently before seeing the answer is not easily convinced that anyone but God is responsible for the results.

An Illustration of Prayer

To illustrate real prayer, Jesus provided an example. His prayer, commonly known as the Lord's Prayer, contained little that a Pharisee might not have prayed. The Eighteen Benedictions of the rabbis, for example, referred to God as Father, asked that His name be kept holy, prayed that His rule might extend throughout the earth, and petitioned God for forgiveness. But anyone who has ever read the Lord's Prayer and the Eighteen Benedictions quickly recognizes some very important differences.

Jesus' prayer contains a personal, intimate dimension unknown to the rabbis' teachings. Jesus' words also exhibit a child-like simplicity that differs sharply from the studied phrases and formal expressions of the Jewish leaders. Obviously, the model prayer is a classic example of brevity that is only possible for one who recognizes that he's praying to a God who already knows and sees.

Writers and communications specialists have long cited Jesus' words as an example of clear, to-the-point prose. A writer in *Letter Perfect,* a communications newsletter, observes that many people think that the more words one uses, the better. He suggests that today, many teachers would tell their disciples to say,

> We respectfully petition, request, and entreat that due and adequate provision be made, this day and the date hereinafter subscribed, for the satisfying of this petitioner's nutritional requirements and for the organizing of such methods as may be deemed necessary and proper to assure the reception by and for said petitioner of such quantities of baked cereal products as shall, in the judgment of the aforesaid petitioners, constitute a sufficient supply thereof.

Jesus taught His followers to simply say, "Give us this day our daily bread."

The Desires of the Heart

Jesus' model prayer contains six petitions that reveal the true desires of the disciple's heart. The disciple begins by recognizing that he is speaking to his Heavenly Father, not a reluctant god that must be overwhelmed and persuaded to listen. He prays from a relationship of love and confidence.

The first three petitions focus on God and the second three on the needs of the disciple:

Hallowed be your name. God's name refers to His person and character, all that He is and stands for. *Hallowed* speaks of setting something apart, giving it a special place. The disciple's greatest desire is to see God worshiped and honored as He alone deserves.

Your kingdom come. The kingdom of God is His rule. The Jews of Jesus' day would have prayed this prayer thinking of the coming of the Messiah's earthly, political reign. Jesus taught that the kingdom was coming, but in a way that few had expected. He came to introduce the rule of God in the lives of believers who lived in the *midst of the world.*

Eventually all of the universe will once again come under the absolute rule of God (1 Corinthians 15:20-28). Now it is a kingdom within a kingdom. The kingdom of God in the world is surrounded by the kingdom of the world. In a sense, the kingdom has come in the resurrection of Jesus and the coming of the Holy Spirit. In another sense, it is still coming as the gospel is spread and accepted by one person after another. In yet another sense, the kingdom awaits its final coming when Jesus returns to take His rightful place as sovereign over the entire universe.

Your will be done on earth as it is in heaven. This echoes the concern of the previous petition. God's rule is His will. His kingdom is where that will is followed and obeyed. The true desire of the disciple is that God's will might be as perfectly obeyed on earth as it is in His presence in Heaven.

Before the disciple ever turns his attention to his own needs, he prays for the rule of God in the world. His vision extends beyond the limits of his own experience. His love is for God, not self.

Give us today our daily bread. The prayer for daily bread comes from the heart of faith. The disciple knows that God is his source of supply. Living day by day in the knowledge that God cares and provides is the greatest security possible. It teaches one to remember what Moses said of the manna God had provided for Israel, "Man does not live on bread alone but on every word that comes from the mouth of the Lord" (Deuteronomy 8:3).

Forgive us our debts, as we also have forgiven our debtors. Only the blindest of hypocrites can stand in the presence of God and not be overwhelmed by his own sinfulness (Luke 18:9-14). Only the most ungrateful can receive the forgiving grace of God and refuse to pass that same blessing on (Matthew 18:21-35).

And lead us not into temptation, but deliver us from the evil one. The disciple knows that just as he depends upon God for his physical survival, he also requires God's blessing for his spiritual and moral well-being. Faith has no room for self-confidence that sees itself as invulnerable to temptation or evil. This petition belongs to the poor in spirit.

Older translations of the prayer contain a closing doxology. Bible scholars now believe that this was not a part of the original, for it is not in the better copies of Matthew's Gospel. Many think that sometime centuries after the writing of the Gospel, the words "for thine is the kingdom, and the power, and the glory forever" were added when the prayer began to be used as a part of the church's formal ritual.

Jesus concluded the discussion of prayer not with a doxology but with a reminder of the place of forgiveness (Matthew 6:14-15). He wanted to remind His disciples once again that one's relationship to God and his relationship to those around him are intimately connected. The capacity to forgive and the experience of forgiveness are twin graces.

In these six petitions (for God's name, His kingdom, His will, our food, our forgiveness, and our future protection), Jesus includes the whole of human experience. Prayer is all inclusive. Everything that rightfully belongs to the disciple's life belongs in his prayers. Anything that cannot be prayed about ought to be eliminated. Prayer also covers every dimension of the disciple's relationship with God. It is more than asking; it is communication.

Some Practical Questions

No discussion of these words on prayer is complete without considering a few practical questions.

Should this model prayer be recited as a part of the church's public worship? Some churches do so every Lord's Day. Others argue that to repeat these words over and over again violates the very lesson Jesus was teaching. Certainly, to use the model prayer as a substitute for heart-felt personal prayer is not what Jesus had in mind. He provided an example, not a magic formula that was to be repeated. However, the public reading or reciting of this or any other passage of Scripture can be a meaningful part of public worship.

Does Jesus' admonition about retreating to a closet to pray rule out public prayer? The reference to praying in a closet or closed room is best understood as a figure of speech. Jesus was warning against praying to be seen of men. One can pray in a closet with the same effect. One need only mark it "Prayer Room" and make sure that others see him enter. Public prayer can violate the teaching of Jesus if it is done to exhibit one's piety rather than to lead the congregation to God's throne. Both Jesus and the early church prayed publicly (Matthew 26:26; Luke 11:1; John 17:1-26; Acts 1:14; 3:11; 4:24-31).

Is it wrong to pray repeatedly for the same thing? Jesus' warning against "vain repetitions" (Matthew 6:7, KJV) was aimed at those who attempted to manipulate God through meaningless babble or complex ritual. This lies at the heart of nearly all pagan concepts of prayer. On the other hand, Jesus taught His disciples to be persistent in prayer (Luke 11:5-13; Luke 18:1-8). He was most concerned about one's motive for prayer, not the length or content of the petitions.

In the garden, Jesus prayed for the same concern at least three times (Matthew 26:44). Paul prayed three times for release from the "thorn in [his] flesh" only to learn that God had another solution for his plight (2 Corinthians 12:7-9).

102

Making Hell Tremble

Satan will do anything to keep a Christian from prayer. He knows that through prayer, the believer enters into a communion and finds a strength for which Hell is no match. In his solitary prayer closet, the disciple can intercede for another a thousand miles away. He can lift the burdens of those he has never seen. His prayer, unseen by men but heard by God, can open doors for the gospel and target the resources of God where most needed. Faithful prayer can bring healing to the sick, freedom to the captive, and hope to lives darkened by despair. It is the believer's most potent resource and Satan's greatest enemy.

Hell trembles most at the sight of a Christian in prayer!

Chapter Ten

Hungry for God
Matthew 6:16-18

Jesus' list of "righteous acts" included three religious activities. He assumed that His disciples would do all three. *"When* you do this," He said, not *"if."* He assumed that each could be done in a right or wrong manner and that positive benefits (rewards) could be attained by doing them in the right way for the right motive.

Today, alms-giving and praying still head almost everyone's list of Christian activities. But fasting is another matter! Many consider this practice a relic of the past or, at best, something that only the most pious fanatic does. Few would place it in the same context as giving and praying as Jesus did. Perhaps Jesus knew something that the modern church has forgotten!

Fasting in the Old Testament

The Biblical terms for fasting describe an abstinence from food and/or drink for an undetermined period of time. A fast could last for a day or as long as several weeks. The term was used to describe a voluntary action or forced hunger (as in the case of a famine or a military seige). Even the cattle of Ninevah were described as fasting when the king declared a period of mourning and repentance (Jonah 3:5-9). Paul used the same term to refer to the hunger he experienced in his service of Christ (2 Corinthians 6:5; 11:27).

A fast might include the total abstinence from food or it could be partial. Daniel refused the king's meat and wine for three weeks while he mourned the fate of his people (Daniel 10:2, 3). Moses and Jesus both fasted from all food for forty days and forty nights.

The Jewish law required that all Israel observe one annual fast, the Day of Atonement (Leviticus 23:27). After the exile, the Jews held four annual fasts to remind the nation of their suffering during the captivity.

Many individuals and groups in Jewish history fasted for a variety of reasons. The entire nation fasted and offered sacrifices as they sought direction from God for battle (Judges 20:26). When they learned of the death of Saul, the people of Jabesh-Gilead fasted for a week (1 Samuel 31:13). David and his men fasted for a full day upon learning of the same event (2 Samuel 1:12).

When David prayed for the life of his child, he fasted for seven days (2 Samuel 12:16-23). Jehoshaphat called upon all of Judah to fast during a time of national emergency (2 Chronicles 20:3). Nehemiah prayed and fasted for days out of concern for the fate of the Jewish exiles (Nehemiah 1:4). Hannah prayed and refused to eat when she asked God to provide her a son (1 Samuel 1:7, 8). Esther, her hand-maidens, and her fellow Jews fasted for three days as the queen prepared to go before the king and intercede for her people (Esther 4:16).

Several other activities frequently accompanied a fast. Men tore their clothes, put ashes on their heads, or dressed in sackcloth. Most often those who fasted also prayed and wept.

Humbling the Soul

The purposes of the fast varied with the occasion. Culturally, fasting was a sign of mourning and often accompanied the death of a loved one or a national leader. Fasting also expressed humiliation and a sense of dependence on God. The Day of Atonement reminded Israel of the need for forgiveness. The Old Testament used the phrases "afflicting the body" or "afflicting the soul" to describe the act of self-denial involved in fasting. David said, "I humbled my soul with fasting" (Psalm 35:13, NASB).

As a companion of prayer, fasting intensified the petitioner's quest for the help and guidance of God. The psalmist alludes to this when he testifies, "My soul thirsts for God, for the living God. When can I go and meet with God? My tears have been my food day and night" (Psalm 42:2, 3). In desperation for the plight of Israel, Daniel "turned to the Lord God and pleaded with him in prayer and petition, in fasting, and in sackcloth and ashes" (Daniel 9:3). Fasting demonstrated the sincerity of the believer and enabled him to concentrate more completely on the matter at hand, seeking God.

The Abuse of Fasting

Long before the time of the Pharisees, fasting was abused. Jeremiah insisted that even though they fasted, God would not hear the cries of Judah (Jeremiah 14:12). Zechariah accused the priests and leaders of fasting for themselves and not to God (Zechariah 7:5, 6). Isaiah provided the most ringing rebuke of false fasting. The people, he said, had sought God but not done His will. Fasting was more than a pious ritual, the prophet insisted. It was to be accompanied by righteousness and justice or it meant nothing.

Listen to Isaiah's stirring call to God-centered fasting:

> For day after day they seek me out;
>> they seem eager to know my ways,
> as if they were a nation that does what is right
>> and has not forsaken the commands of its God.
> They ask me for just decisions
>> and seem eager for God to come near them.
> "Why have we fasted," they say,
>> "and you have not seen it?
> "Why have we humbled ourselves,
>> and you have not noticed?"
>
> Yet on the day of your fasting, you do as you please
>> and exploit all your workers.
> Your fasting ends in quarreling and strife,
>> and in striking each other with wicked fists.
> You cannot fast as you do today
>> and expect your voice to be heard on high.
> Is this the kind of fast I have chosen,
>> only a day for a man to humble himself?
> Is it only for bowing one's head like a reed
>> and for lying on sackcloth and ashes?
> Is that what you call a fast,
>> a day acceptable to the Lord?
>
> Is not this the kind of fasting I have chosen:
>> to loose the chains of injustice
>> and untie the cords of the yoke,
> to set the oppressed free
>> and break every yoke?

Is it not to share your food with the hungry
  and to provide the poor wanderer with shelter—
when you see the naked, to clothe him,
  and not to turn away from your own flesh and blood?
Then your light will break forth like the dawn,
  and your healing will quickly appear;
then your righteousness will go before you,
  and the glory of the Lord will be your rear guard.
Then you will call, and the Lord will answer.
  you will cry for help, and he will say: Here am I (Isaiah 58:2-9).

Fasting in the New Testament

By the time of the New Testament, fasting had become an important part of Jewish religion. The Pharisees fasted twice a week, on Monday and Thursday. John the Baptist and his disciples also fasted regularly (Matthew 9:14; Mark 2:18; Luke 5:33). Fasting was such an assumed part of Jewish piety that John's disciples considered it odd that Jesus' disciples did not fast as they did. Jesus explained that as a sign of mourning, fasting was inappropriate for those who enjoyed the presence of the bridegroom. "The time will come when the bridegroom will be taken from them;" he said, "then they will fast" (Matthew 9:15). Even though Jesus' disciples did not fast regularly as did their contemporaries, Jesus assumed that the time would come when they would.

In fact, the early church did fast. It was while the leaders of the Antioch church were worshiping and fasting that the Holy Spirit revealed the instructions that Saul and Barnabas be set apart to carry the gospel to other lands (Acts 13:2). Fasting and prayer took place again as the men were sent off on their work (Acts 13:3). Paul and Barnabas followed this same tradition when they set apart elders in the churches they had planted. They "appointed elders for them in each church and, with prayer and fasting, committed them to the Lord, in whom they had put their trust" (Acts 14:23).

Hypocritical Fasting

As with the other "acts of righteousness" practiced by the Pharisees, Jesus did not condemn fasting but the abuse of it. The hypocrites gave alms, prayed, and fasted with the same goal in mind—to be seen of men. What had originally been an act of humiliation had been turned into a token of religious pride. When the saints of the Old Testament fasted, they confessed their sinfulness before God. The hypocrites attempted to announce their self-righteousness through the same act.

To insure that no one overlooked their piety, those Jesus denounced took great care to "show men" they were fasting (Matthew 6:16). Jesus used an interesting play on words to describe their actions. "They disfigure their faces to show men they are fasting," He said. The terms *disfigure* and *show* are opposites or antonyms in the original language. Jesus said they "hid" in order "to show," or "concealed" so they could "reveal." Their strategy worked. Everyone knew how religious the Pharisees were. But as with their prayers and alms-giving, Jesus insisted that their human audiences were the only ones impressed. God was not. The only reward they could expect for their fasting was the attention they received.

Rather than instructing His disciples not to fast at all, Jesus explained an alternative. He advocated secret fasting. When they gave alms, they were to not let their left hand know what their right hand was doing. When they prayed, He told them to go into a closet and shut the door. When they fasted, they were to do everything possible to appear normal. Instead of wearing sackcloth and ashes, He told them to wash their faces and annoint their heads with oil as they would on any other day. At issue was not just how they dressed when they fasted, but their motive. Every "act of righteousness" was to be done before God and not men.

The Lost Discipline

Since fasting was so common in the Old Testament and practiced in the New Testament, it is strange that so little has been said of it in the modern church. John Stott says of Jesus' instructions on fasting in the Sermon on the Mount that we "live our lives as if such scriptures have been removed from our Bible." One reason for the great silence about fasting may be the fact that materialism and self-fulfillment so dominate the spirit of our world. At the turn of the century, D. R. Dungan observed that fasting contradicted the most basic life-style of most Americans. In 1902, in an article on fasting in the *Christian Evangelist,* he wrote, "If the American people are conspicuous for any one characteristic it is the habit of eating regularly and as much as they want."

The ease with which many separate the spiritual and the physical has also contributed to the demise of fasting. Few see any relationship between the experience of the body and the enrichment of the spirit. In Scripture, the two were intimately related. While Jesus and the whole of the New Testament rejected the tendency to define spirituality in terms of eating or not eating certain foods (Colossians 2:20-23; Romans 14:17, 18; Mark 7:19), they left room for fasting as a discipline with spiritual benefits.

The Benefits of Fasting

In recent years, many medical experts have lauded the physical benefits of fasting, provided it is practiced with common sense and moderation. This has put the lie to the argument that a Christian shouldn't fast because of alleged dangers to the body.

Several years ago, a friend shared with me a book that promoted fasting for both physical and spiritual reasons. Prior to that time, I had never fasted or given much thought to it. After reading the book, I became convinced that spiritual and physical well-being are related. I realized that the key to losing weight, which I had needed to do for some time, was greater physical discipline. This physical discipline was, in turn, related to spiritual discipline. Fasting, the author of the book contended, could help break the cycle of undiscipline and lead the way to better health in both areas.

I decided to test the theory. To make a long story short, I fasted for ten days. During that time, I ate and drank nothing but water. The physical experience was exactly what I had read about. For the first two to three days, my stomach growled and I occasionally suffered from hunger-related headaches. By the third day, the sense of hunger and the headaches both abated as my body adjusted to internal combustion. About the only adverse sensation I experienced for the next three or four days was extreme fatigue. I felt much as I had on those rare occasions when I had gone without sleep for a day or two. By the time I broke the fast on the tenth day, my energy level had rebounded back to something closer to normal. During the ten days, I lost several pounds and experienced a genuine sense of physical refreshment.

I also benefited from some spiritual rewards as well. I didn't see visions or hear voices, but I learned some lessons about the Lord and His relationship to my total life that I had needed to learn. First, I learned some facts about food. I realized how much of a food-addict I had become. The physical body actually needs very little food to function well. I, like many, had grown accustomed to "living to eat," rather than "eating to live." After fasting for several days, I vowed I would never again complain that I was "starving to death" simply because I failed to eat a second doughnut at coffee break.

I also learned something about the social dimensions of eating. Scripture speaks of spiritual and human fellowship in terms of "breaking bread" together. When I didn't eat, I missed more than a few meals. I also missed the interaction and human intimacy that comes with sharing food. The Lord's table took on added meaning.

The experience of fasting also taught me a great appreciation for my body and its health. In many ways, fasting was not a pleasant experience. I was tired. My body ached. I knew I couldn't do everything I was accustomed to doing. I grew thankful that my physical limitations were only temporary. I could drink a glass of juice or eat a bowl of soup and be as good as new within an hour. But I thought of the millions of people, some that I knew, whose physical problems were not going to go away as easily as that. I was reminded of the fact that countless people were experiencing the same symptoms I was because of famine, not fasting. I was determined never again to take "my daily bread" for granted.

I can't describe how good food tasted when I finally started eating again. Simple things like a cold glass of tomato juice or a crisp bite of celery exploded in my mouth with unexpected flavor. Suddenly, the quality of food, rather than the quantity, became important. I ate slower, savoring each new flavor and aroma. Simple things became objects of thanksgiving.

The Spiritual Rewards of Fasting

Looking back, I think the most significant result of my experiment in fasting was spiritual. I did pray and study the Scriptures a bit more than normal during the ten-day fast. But other spiritual benefits far outstripped these activities. During the fast, I gained a new appreciation for the fact that my life is always dependent on God in every way. I saw anew the frailty of life. I came to see that God indeed is my source of strength. When I eliminated the false security of physical energy and nourishment, I saw more clearly how intensely I needed the spiritual sustenance that only God could provide. Even though my prayer life didn't increase greatly in quantity during the fast, I am convinced it improved in quality. As my physical energy diminished, my spiritual energy increased.

I wouldn't advise anyone else to do what I did. In retrospect, I think the ten-day fast was a bit extreme. I haven't repeated the experience, although I wouldn't necessarily rule it out for the future. I have, however, fasted for shorter periods of time (two or three days on several occasions and for a week at least twice). Each time, I have found that both physical and spiritual benefits are still present.

A word of caution is perhaps needed at this point. From a physical standpoint, fasting is serious business. No one with health problems should attempt even a short fast without proper medical advice. Even the healthy should begin gradually. A partial fast in which only juice is taken provides a good starting point. Anything beyond a two-or three-day fast should be approached very cautiously. Ending the fast is also quite critical. One can't simply begin eating normally again after a fast of several days without experiencing some very unpleasant and potentially dangerous side effects.

More Than Food

Richard Foster, in his book *Celebration of Discipline,* suggests that the principle of fasting can be applied to things other than food. Foster defines fasting as "the voluntary denial of an otherwise normal function for the sake of intense spiritual activity." The emphasis is upon the "voluntary denial" of what is otherwise right and proper. The motive is not to impress others with our piety and faith, but to draw closer to God and learn valuable spiritual lessons.

Consider some of the "normal functions" that could be temporarily denied with great benefit:

People. Sometimes we need just to get away from the hustle and bustle of the crowd as Jesus did after His baptism. Solitude can be spiritually refreshing.

Noise. The constant din of the radio or television can keep us distracted from the more personal spiritual issues of our lives. Quietness so intense that we can "hear ourselves think" also provides opportunity for God to work.

Clocks. Most of us are so time conscious that we are virtually enslaved by our watches. Much of it is self-imposed. Often our rush to keep our artificial schedules leaves no time for the things of the Spirit.

Shopping. Our consumer culture equates living with buying. People purchase items they don't need with money they don't have. A year later they resell the same things at garage sales to other people who don't need them either. Forcing ourselves to learn to be satisfied with what we have and to buy only what we need are valuable experiences for most of us. As Jesus noted in the next section of the Sermon on the Mount, this *is* a spiritual matter!

Affluence. Our infatuation with collecting more and more things cannot be separated from the contagion of wealth. The more we have, the more we want. Eventually, the cycle leads to idolatry, the worship of the gifts rather than the Giver. Voluntarily giving our wealth to the poor is a spiritual exercise, especially if we learn to trust in God and not gold in the process.

Hungry for Righteousness

Jesus may have had more than a passing connection in mind when he linked alms-giving, prayer, and fasting. In giving, we voluntarily share our abundance with those in need. In prayer, we declare our devotion to God's kingdom and our dependence on His provision. Fasting combines elements of both. It makes more of what we have available for alms-giving and at the same time teaches us to depend on God.

Alms-giving, prayer, and fasting demand that a person clarify his priorities. Once this is done properly, the rewards are guaranteed.

"Blessed are those who hunger and
thirst for righteousness,
for they will be filled."

Chapter Eleven

The Weeds of the Spirit
Matthew 6:19-34

It's confession time!

I grew up on a farm in central Illinois. Because the farm was quite small, Dad almost always held down at least one other full-time job to make enough money to finance his farming habit.

As the eldest son on that kind of farming operation, I learned the facts of farm life at a very early age. I did a little of everything. When I was tall enough to reach the pedals, I learned to drive a tractor. I can remember carrying feed and water to the hogs early in the morning before going to school. In the summer, I helped fill the barn with hay. In the winter, we emptied it. A lot of it was hard work. Some of it was fun.

But there was one part of farm work that I dreaded more than anything else. It wasn't milking the cows, even though dodging a reluctant bovine's feet and tail was no small task. Even cleaning out the barn on a hot summer day, as unpleasant as that could be, was better, as far as I was concerned, than walking beans.

In case you never had the pleasure of growing up on a Midwestern farm, let me explain what "walking beans" is all about. Soy beans, along with corn, is one of the staple crops of grain farms in Illinois and much of the Midwest. As with other crops, controlling weeds in the beans is a major concern for farmers. Today, a variety of chemical herbicides are used either to kill the weeds or, better yet, to prevent them from sprouting. But not when I was growing up.

Even if the chemicals had been available, however, my father and most of the farmers I knew would still have argued that the best weed killer was a boy with a hoe. So for several weeks each summer, my brothers and I were assigned the daily task of walking through acre after acre of bean fields, cutting and hoeing weeds as we went.

At least, that's what we were supposed to do.

More often, we would work hardest at finding an excuse for not going to the fields that day. We were certain that on any given day, it was either too hot, too cold, too wet, or too dry! Eventually, the fields would get patrolled. But most of the work was accomplished in the evenings or on weekends when Dad was there to set the pace and encourage us to get to work.

Even to this day, pulling weeds is far from my favorite activity. I enjoy planting a garden. Picking tomatoes, pulling onions, or even digging potatoes is fun. But the real work comes in mid-summer when the weeds and I fight it out for control of that little patch of real estate. Don't bother to ask who wins. Someday I am hoping for a draw!

The Problem With Weeds

Why all the fuss about weeds? I didn't always understand it as a kid growing up on a farm. But even as a less-than-successful gardener, today I know that the greater the weeds, the less the harvest. Weeds and a truly fruitful crop cannot co-exist. It's either one or the other.

What does all of this have to do with the life of a disciple? According to Jesus, everything!

Jesus insisted that a fruitful life of righteousness was not an automatic matter. Many obstacles confront the believer that can subvert the faith before it ever has a chance to produce results.

Listen to the way Jesus described this fact of faith in his parable of the sower:

> A farmer went out to sow his seed. As he was scattering the seed, some fell along the path, and the birds came and ate it up. Some fell on rocky places, where it did not have much soil. It sprang up quickly, because the soil was shallow. But when the sun came up, the plants were scorched, and they withered because they had no root. Other seed fell among thorns, which grew up and choked the plants (Matthew 13:3-7).

What I find most interesting is Jesus' explanation of the thorns. If I were explaining the story, I would have equated the thorns that choked the life from the faith with such noxious problems as lust, intemperate behavior, or a host of other personal and social ills. But note how Jesus defines the weed-filled life.

> The one who received the seed that fell among the thorns is the man who hears the word, but the worries of this life and the deceitfulness of wealth choke it, making it unfruitful (Matthew 13:22).

Does this have anything to do with us? You bet it does! Jesus pulls no punches. He makes it clear that one of the major problems that undermines a fruitful, faith-filled life for a disciple is money and our attitude toward it.

Not long ago, *Money Magazine* conducted a major survey entitled "Americans and Their Money." The 2065-page report was based on a sampling of nearly 2500 adult men and women. Among other things, the researchers concluded that a vast majority of Americans spend a great deal of time thinking about money. The report stated that "everyone appears to be preoccupied with money matters to some degree, but a key difference is that higher income people are more concerned with investments, while the poor are thinking about how to pay their bills."

If this is true, and I think it is, we have a "weed-control" problem. What Jesus identified 2000 years ago as a major obstacle to a righteous and godly life is still with us today. The "worries of this life" (how to pay our bills) or the "deceitfulness of wealth" (a preoccupation with the right investments) are issues that every disciple who wants a fruitful life must confront.

Money Is a Spiritual Matter

This fact brings us to our next section in the Sermon on the Mount. At first, it may appear that Matthew 6:19 introduces a major shift in subject matter. This is only partly true. The previous section outlined Jesus' call for a sincere religion that left no room for a phony, counterfeit faith that sought to impress others with outlandish demonstrations of false piety. Jesus demanded heart-faith.

In this new section, Christ turned His attention to another problem of the heart. Hypocritical religion seeks to produce fruit from an empty heart. A money-centered life endeavors to do it from a cluttered heart. Both fail. Both problems undermine true faith and genuine discipleship.

Before we can understand what Jesus had to say here, we first need to straighten out some of the mixed-up thinking that often influences our attitudes toward God and our money. Note three facts.

115

First, *God doesn't need our money.* He is the creator and sustainer of all. He already owns everything. Any view of money and possessions that sees God in a dependent relationship to us is completely confused.

Second, *God is not a tight-fisted Scrooge* whose goal is to keep His subjects from enjoying life. Nor is God indifferent to the needs of His creation. Jesus made it clear that the Father wants to provide for His children. Meeting the spiritual, emotional, and material needs of His worshipers is God's specialty.

Finally, *money is not ethically and morally neutral.* The use or abuse of our possessions is a highly spiritual matter, every bit as spiritual as prayer and fasting. In fact, few other areas of our lives have as much potential to impact our faith as does money. Jesus recognized this. This fact alone explains why He spent more time teaching His would-be followers about the proper attitude toward money than about nearly any other topic. Unless we understand this fact, we will never understand what Jesus says next in this primer on discipleship.

Matthew 6:19-34 presents Jesus' guidelines for eliminating those weeds of the Spirit that can easily choke out the fruit of faith. In this section, He addressed two distinct groups of people. Each of us is represented in one or the other of the groups. He speaks first to what I call the "haves" and then to the "have nots".

A Word to the Haves (Matthew 6:19-24)

Jesus first addressed the plight of those who are rich and want to stay that way. According to the *Money* survey, the main preoccupation of today's rich is with finding the right investments. Like a good financial counselor, Jesus pointed His clients to the best place to put their wealth for the greatest return. He cautioned against risky, unsure ventures and explained in the clearest of terms the consequences of making the wrong choices.

Unlike most financial planners, Jesus' advice to the wealthy took into account issues that went beyond the normal concerns for an adequate retirement income and family security. He counseled in terms of spiritual interest that could be compounded into eternal dividends.

Jesus' advice to the wealthy centers on three key word-pictures.

He first spoke in terms of *treasure.* He contrasted temporal, insecure earthly treasure with the totally safe Heavenly investments. No one but a fool or a crook would buy stock in a company he knew was headed for bankruptcy. One might buy a brick of gold in hopes that the price would go up, but no one would put all his money in a block of ice that would melt before he could get it home.

That's the very picture Jesus painted of the wealthy who treat their money as if it were their most valuable asset in life.

Jesus next talked of *light and sight*. Wealth is really a matter of value and priority. A person lives for that at which he aims. Aim in the wrong direction, and success becomes disaster.

Finally, He put money matters in the most radical terms when He linked wealth with *slavery*. We normally associate riches with freedom. A wealthy man can do anything he wants, we think. Think again, Jesus has warned. Riches, wrongly regarded, can easily lead to the worst kind of slavery. It comes between a man and his freedom to love and serve God. When a man becomes possessed by his possessions, he is no longer free, no matter how rich he is.

Elsewhere, Jesus illustrated these warnings with the stories of three men, all of whom were haves and all of whom made what would prove to be costly investments. In their preoccupation with keeping their riches, they lost their opportunity for even greater treasure. Each man illustrates a different one of the three key concepts found in Matthew 6:19-24. The first put his treasures in the wrong place. The second was blind to the right values of life. The third was imprisoned by his own success.

The Rich Fool (Luke 12:13-21). Jesus told this story as a warning against covetousness. He intended it to shock a would-be follower back into reality and away from his preoccupation with his bank account.

By every earthly standard, the farmer was a success. His barns were overflowing. His business was expanding. Everything was going his way. But in his race to accumulate more and more wealth, he made some major miscalculations. His friends may have considered him a shrewd business manager, but God labeled him a fool.

What made him a fool? First, he forgot *the real values of life*. He thought his wealth was the key to life. Like many in our materialistically-bent society, he was convinced that the accumulation of wealth was the highest good. The root of all evil, he might have thought, was the lack, not the love, of money.

Earlier in this century, a young man named Roger Morgan left the poverty of the Appplachian Mountains to make his fortune in the big city. With a single-minded purpose, Morgan made money his total preoccupation. It worked. Within a few years, he was worth millions.

Then came the crash of 1929 and the Great Depression that followed. His fortune evaporated and Morgan was again reduced to poverty. Penniless, he took to the road as a hobo.

One day, a friend found Morgan on the Golden Gate Bridge staring down into the waters of the Bay. When the friend suggested that they move on, Morgan resisted. "Leave me alone," he replied, "I'm trying to think. There is something more important than money, but I've forgotten what it is."

The rich farmer also forgot that whatever value money may have, *it all vanishes at death.* As Paul reminds us, "We brought nothing into the world, and we can take nothing out of it" (1 Timothy 6:7). No man dies rich. At the moment of death, he looses every possession he owns. The Egyptians buried their treasure with them in their graves so they could take it to the other side. But despite all of the preparation, their riches remained behind for thieves and rust.

The rich farmer needed to hear the reminder of Isaiah. The prophet pointed to the Lord and said, "He will be the sure foundation for your times, a rich store of salvation and wisdom and knowledge; the fear of the Lord is the key to this treasure" (Isaiah 33:6).

The Rich Blind Man (Luke 16:19-31). Jesus' story of the rich man and Lazarus takes His teachings on money a step further. The rich farmer learned the true values of life in the face of death. This rich man in this second parable discovered the same truths after the grave.

Throughout life, he had been blind to the greater treasures of life and to the needs of others. The beggar at his door was an object of charity but not compassion. Only after his death did the rich man suddenly become concerned about others. His entire life had been lived with his sight fixed on one thing. He could see nothing but the accumulation of wealth and the satisfaction of his own pleasures. In the process, he missed the opportunities for true treasure.

Author Gary Freeman tells of a young girl whose life parallels many today. As she was growing up she had one goal—to marry and have children. Eventually, she graduated from high school, married her sweetheart, and had four children.

Unfortunately, she was soon surprised to learn how demanding raising a family of small children could be. "I can't wait until these children are in school, so I can enjoy life," she told her friends.

Finally, when the youngest started school, she and her husband decided that she should go to work so they could save money for the children's college education. She hated working. "I can't wait until the kids finish school so I can quit work," she said.

When the last child was through college, she was in a management position at the factory and had only eight more years to go until she could retire with full benefits. She still didn't like the job but decided to stay with it. "I can't wait till I retire," she said.

She had spent her whole life waiting and looking forward.

Finally, she and her husband retired and moved to Florida. They spent the rest of their years sitting on the front porch of the cottage, leafing through the family album, remembering the "good ol' days."

Too late she discovered how blind she had been. She was always looking ahead to a better day. She lost many of the true joys of life while waiting for the future.

The Rich Slave (Luke 18:18-30). He had everything a yuppie could want. He was rich, young, and powerful. He had it all. But something was missing. Despite all of his success, he wanted something more. He asked Jesus to help him find it.

I don't know what this rich young ruler expected to hear. Whatever it was, Jesus didn't give it to him. The Master's words must have left him stunned. "Sell everything you have and give to the poor, and you will have treasure in heaven. Then come, follow me" (Luke 18:22).

However much he may have wanted to do what Jesus asked, he couldn't. His wealth had a strangle hold on his soul. He was possessed by his own possessions, a slave to his own success. Since he couldn't serve both God and money, he turned his back on Jesus and remained a man with a full purse and an empty heart.

"But I'm Not Rich." Most of us read these words of Jesus, consider the examples of the rich whose faith was choked by their wealth, and then dismiss the teachings. "Some people may have that problem, but not me," we tell ourselves. "I'm not rich!"

This may be our biggest problem with Jesus' words on faith and finances. None of us considers himself rich. If we had a little more, then maybe we might be in danger of substituting our possessions for God. We forget that materialism and covetousness are not a matter of amount, but attitude. Its roots grow from the heart, not the pocketbook.

Yes, we are rich! There may be a few exceptions, but most of you who read these pages *are* so rich in comparison with most of the world that it defies description. Madison Avenue has so completely distorted our needs and wants that we no longer have an accurate picture of our own condition. Perhaps this is the reason Jesus preceeded His discussion of wealth with a lesson on fasting. Only by fasting can the haves actually experience the feelings of the have nots.

Consider the facts: Americans comprise five percent of the world's population, and yet we possess eighty-seven percent of the world's wealth. Half of the world subsists on $300 a year. As a nation, we consume 15% of the world's food supply. The average person among us uses ten times as much oil and forty times as much steel as our neighbors across the sea.

Are you a have or have not? Make no mistake about it. The rest of the world has little difficulty answering that question for you.

A Word to the Have Nots (Matthew 6:25-34)

Jesus next turned His attention to the other weed. The haves of this world may fall prey to the "deceitfulness of riches," but the have not's struggle with the "cares of the world." Both have the same effect. They strangle faith and destroy the fruit of a godly life.

The term Jesus used in His parable of the sower is the same found in the instructions of Matthew 6:25-34. The word is rendered in the King James Version as "take no thought." This unfortunate translation gives the concept a totally different emphasis from that of the Greek word found in the text. The word was used to describe the mental state of anxiety. The plural was often used by the Greeks for the cares of life that disturb sleep.

Jesus was not advocating that His disciples display a thoughtless, irresponsible attitude toward the future. Rather, He was forbidding worry or fear that robs life of its joy and faith of its power. Interestingly, the English term *worry* derives from an older Anglo-Saxon word that literally meant to strangle or choke. This was precisely what Jesus said that the "cares of this world" would do to the seeds of faith!

The Waste of Worry. Jesus' words suggest three reasons why worry and fruitful faith cannot grow in the same heart.

First, worry is *irreverent*. Anxiety about the future is a contradiction of faith and confident trust in the living God. The Lord has promised that He will never leave or forsake us (Hebrews 13:5). That statement is either true or it is not. If it is true and God can be trusted to keep His word, then there is no need for fear-filled worry or anxiety.

John Stott quotes a simple verse that echoes the sentiments of Jesus:

> Said the robin to the sparrow:
> I should really like to know
> Why these anxious human beings
> Rush about and worry so.
>
> Said the sparrow to the robin;
> Friend, I think that it must be
> That they have no heavenly Father,
> Such as cares for you and me.

"Cast all your anxiety on him" exhorts Peter, "because he cares for you" (1 Peter 5:7). David sounds the same note of confidence when he calls the faithful not to "fret because of evil men" but to "trust in the Lord," to "commit your way to the Lord," and to "be still before the Lord and wait patiently for him" (Psalm 37:1, 3, 5, 7).

Worry is *irrelevant*. As one woman put it, "I have had a lot of trouble in life—most of which never happened." Jesus' words on the subject were to the same effect, "Who of you by worrying can add a single hour to his life?" He said (Matthew 6:27).

An article in the *Illinois Medical Journal* offered wise counsel for sound mental and spiritual health when it summed up the pointlessness of undue anxiety.

> There are two days in every week about which we should not worry—two days which should be kept free from fear and apprehension.

One of these days is yesterday, with its mistakes and cares, its aches and pains, its faults and blunders. Yesterday has passed forever beyond our control. All the money in the world cannot bring back yesterday. We cannot erase a single word we said.

The other day we should not worry about is tomorrow, with its possible adversities, its burdens, its large promise and performance. Tomorrow also is beyond our immediate control.

Tomorrow's sun will rise either in splendor or behind a mask of clouds, but it will rise. Until it does, we have no stake in tomorrow, for it is yet unborn.

This leaves only one day—today. Any man can fight the battles of just one day. It is only when you and I add the burdens of these two awful eternities—yesterday and tomorrow—that we are liable to break down."

In Jesus' words, "Do not worry about tomorrow, for tomorrow will worry about itself. Each day has enough trouble of its own" (Matthew 6:34).

Worry is *irresponsible*. Anxiety robs us of the spiritual, physical, and emotional strength that we need to meet the challenges that cause us to worry in the first place. It accomplishes nothing. Instead, it paves the way to the dreaded defeat.

We have all experienced the paralyzing effects of anxiety or depression. Even in its milder forms, it builds a huge spiritual roadblock. Witnessing, praying, studying the Word, even helping a hurting brother are next to impossible once worry gets its grip on us.

Abraham Lincoln liked to refer to what he called the Fox River Rule. He spoke of it often whenever anyone asked what was going to happen to the Union during the early days of the War Between the States. Instead of giving an opinion, Lincoln would tell them a story.

During his young circuit-riding days, Lincoln would recollect, he and his companions were traveling in Northern Illinois during a spring rainy season. Most of the rivers of the region were swollen and presented great difficulty for the horsemen. They knew that the next day they would be forced to ford the much larger Fox River. If the smaller streams were any indication, they knew they were in for trouble.

When they came to an inn where they planned to spend the night, they met a circuit preacher headed in the opposite direction. Evidencing their concern, they asked him about the condition of the Fox.

The wise old preacher responded with a bit of homespun wit. "I know all about the Fox," he said, "I have crossed it often and understand it well. But I have one fixed rule with regard to the Fox River—I never cross it till I reach it!"

James Boice tells of an early Christian convert who was noted for his unswerving faith. His name—Titedios Amenimos—was actually a description given him by the admirers of his confidence in God. His last name meant "not worry." He was known as the man who trusted God rather than worried about the problems of life. No greater compliment could be given a man of God.

Uprooting Worry. The limits of worry may be self evident. But the real problem is what to do about it. Jesus didn't offer a simple solution to our plight. Rather, He simply called us to seek first the kingdom of God and His righteousness. This counsel may be more of an answer than we first recognize.

If worry and anxiety are often the results of disobedience, then their cure may lie in obedience. If we want to overcome fear and replace it with faith, we can find no better starting place than simply to start doing what we know we should do. Tomorrow's faith grows from the Word of God obeyed today. Seeking God's kingdom, wanting His rule in our lives, is the first step toward a victorious faith.

Paul provides additional advice about worry when he writes, "Do not be anxious about anything, but in everything, by prayer and petition, with thanksgiving, present your requests to God. And the peace of God, which transcends all understanding, will guard your hearts and your minds in Christ Jesus" (Philippians 4:6, 7).

Jesus knew that both the haves and the have nots of this world fall victim to the same deceiver. The real issue is not how much we have. The issue is contentment. Many think that simply having more would bring happiness. It may, but not always. The secret is to find contentment first.

Such a perspective is not a cop-out or a rationalization. It is simply an affirmation that "a man's life does not consist in the abundance of his possessions" (Luke 12:15). If this is true, a man is a fool to settle for mere wealth!

Chapter Twelve

The Dangers of Serious Religion
Matthew 7:1-12

If Jesus made one thing clear in the Sermon on the Mount, it is this. He wants His disciples to take their faith seriously. No half-hearted, uncommitted followers need apply. He told them to "seek first his kingdom and his righteousness" (Matthew 6:33). Unless their righteousness exceeded that of the scribes and Pharisees, they had no place in the kingdom (Matthew 5:20). He offered no alternatives, no easier road.

Jesus called fishermen and farmers, tax collectors and temple priests alike to total, uncompromising allegiance to God. He left no room for playing religion. It was all or nothing.

"If anyone comes to me," He warned, "and does not hate his father and mother, his wife and children, his brothers and sisters—yes, even his own life—he cannot be my disciple. And anyone who does not carry his cross and follow me cannot be my disciple" (Luke 14:26, 27).

Later, Jesus laid this same call to total commitment before a congregation of professed believers in the city of Laodicea. In a vision to John, the Lord announced, "I know your deeds, that you are neither cold nor hot. I wish you were either one or the other. So because you are lukewarm—neither hot nor cold—I am about to spit you out of my mouth" (Revelation 3:15, 16).

Jesus wants people who are serious about following him!

The Leaven of the Pharisees

But be warned! There are some dangers that come with serious religion. Jesus implied as much when He told His disciples to "be on guard against the yeast of the Pharisees and Sadducees" (Matthew 16:5-12). He wasn't cautioning them against a certain kind of barley loaf they might buy at the local market. He wanted them to be absolutely committed to His teachings, as these other religious zealots were to theirs, but without their mistakes.

As we have noted elsewhere, the Pharisees, the scribes, and the Sadducees were not religious villians to most in their day. They were committed Jewish believers who took their faith seriously. The Pharisees, especially, were determined to live a life of uncompromising commitment to God. They likely would have spoken in the same kind of radical terms with which Jesus challenged His disciples.

However, something went wrong, as far as Jesus was concerned. The serious religion of the Pharisees turned sour. They used their faith as a club with which to browbeat those with whom they disagreed. Jesus painted them as pompous, self-righteous hypocrites who had to keep on their religious masks to protect their reputations. But behind the masks were empty lives filled with hate and pride. The Pharisees had a reputation to live up to. But God was not impressed!

The Pharisees Live!

Unfortunately, the yeast of the Pharisees is still available. The modern church still has its share of serious Christians who, as Jonathan Swift said, "have just enough religion to make them hate, but not enough to make them love one another." Or as James Boice recalls, "A person said to me, 'If the devil is not able to destroy a Christian's witness by making him apathetic, he will try to do it by making him a fanatic.'" In fact, if we were honest, most of us would have to admit that the very phrase "serious religion" that I have been using brings to mind some negative images. We picture red-faced Bible-thumpers, long on hate and short on compassion, sentencing sinners to Hell and enjoying every minute of it. Fanaticism is not a virtue for most of us.

Yet, Jesus called His disciples to total, uncompromising allegiance! How do we reconcile these conflicting concepts—His call for seriousness on one hand, and His warning against Phariseeism on the other. In other words, is it possible to be a committed disciple without turning into a narrow-minded, hypocritical Pharisee?

Of course it is! And this is exactly what Jesus dealt with as He began to draw the Sermon on the Mount to its conclusion. It is important to see this section (Matthew 7:1-11) in its context.

Stumbling Blocks on the Straight and Narrow

Most consider this the final part of the main body of the sermon. As we noted earlier, Jesus set forth His theme in Matthew 5:20 with His call for exceeding righteousness. He called for an inner holiness that went beyond mere outward show. Both ends of this main discourse are bracketed with a reference to the fulfillment of the Law and the Prophets (Matthew 5:17; 7:12). In between, He outlined the kind of life the whole of Scripture (Law and Prophets) calls for. He touched on everything from righteousness to riches, from prayer and fasting to lust and lying.

The section that begins with what we refer to as chapter 7 at first appears to be a series of unrelated admonitions. Upon a closer examination, however, these form distinct sections that belong together. They form a needed counter-balance to what came before and to the tough challenge that concludes the message.

In these four diverse teachings, Jesus outlined four different dangers that any disciple faces who desires to become serious about his faith. Ironically, the more serious a disciple seeks to become, the more susceptible he is to one or more of these problems. You might call these stumbling blocks on the straight and narrow. Satan uses them to trip the believer in his walk of faith.

Inconsistency: Living a Double Standard (Matthew 7:1-5)

"Do not judge, or you too will be judged" (Matthew 7:1). These words have become the occasion for all sorts of religious confusion. In fact, they may be among the most misunderstood and misapplied in the entire Sermon on the Mount. Before examining what Jesus was teaching, consider what He did not mean.

First, His words are not an argument against police, law courts, or government. As strange as it may seem, some have used these teachings to call for a complete abandonment of any kind of criminal or judicial system. After all, the argument goes, if judging someone else is wrong, it is certainly wrong to arrest, convict, and imprison another human being.

This line of reasoning completely misses the context of Jesus' teachings. As we shall see, His concern was with personal relationships, not social order. Elsewhere, Jesus clearly recognized the right of human governments to exist and exercise their authority (Matthew 22:15-22). Paul affirmed that God used governments, even pagan authorities, to punish evil and maintain justice (Romans 13:1-7).

Second, Jesus' condemnation of judging does not provide a case for moral and spiritual relativism. Simply put, relativism maintains that objective standards of right and wrong or orthodoxy and heresy do not exist. Given such a view, all positions become equally valid, even actions or doctrines that are mutually exclusive.

Sadly, much modern religion is nothing but thinly disguised relativism. Evil behavior has for many become an alternative lifestyle or a social maladjustment, but not sin. Immorality has been defined out of existence. False doctrine, even that which denies the very heart of the Christian faith, has become tolerable because, it is argued, no one has the right to judge another.

Whatever Jesus meant, He was not advocating that kind of a scheme of things. His words on love, hate, lust, honesty, and nearly every other topic in the Sermon on the Mount assumes a standard of right and wrong. (See, for example Matthew 5:21-48.) In the closing section of the discourse, He called for His disciples to distinguish false from true prophets (Matthew 7:15-23). The difference between the false and true was a matter of actions and of behavior, as well as doctrine and false preaching. In a world without moral standards, such words mean nothing.

The rest of the New Testament also assumes a world where right and wrong exist and are knowable. Although Paul also taught Christians not to judge, apparently basing his teachings on these instructions of Jesus (Romans 14:4, 13-18), he could at the same time challenge believers to take a stand against immorality. "I have already passed judgment on the one who did this," he wrote of a man who had scandalized the faith in pagan Corinth by living in open immorality (1 Corinthians 5:3). Paul not only condemned the behavior, he called for other Christians to do the same.

Was this a breech of Jesus' warning against judging? Clearly not in Paul's mind.

Finally, not judging does not mean that disciples of Jesus are to maintain a *laisez faire,* live and let live, attitude toward the world about them. While few Bible-believing Christians would seriously advocate an anarchist or even a relativistic approach to morality, many are reluctant to take strong moral stands against the tide of evil flooding modern society. Whether the issue is abortion, pornography, alcohol abuse, or child abuse, there are always those who contend that believers should keep quiet. "After all," they frequently insist, "Jesus said we are not to judge."

Such attitudes can even infect the evangelistic zeal of Christians. We dare not become too aggressive about telling people that they need Christ, we are told. We can't judge!

If declaring the good news of Jesus to a lost world is judging, then judge we must! Jesus' marching orders to His faithful church were to preach the whole gospel to the whole world (Matthew 28:18-20). That every disciple was to believe that only in Christ are men saved and to make that belief known to the world is assumed on every page of the New Testament.

Believers were told to be compassionate but zealous in attempting to lead sinners from evil to righteousness. James makes it clear:

> My brothers, if one of you should wander from the truth and someone should bring him back, remember this: "Whoever turns a sinner from the error of his way will save him from death and cover over a multitude of sins" (James 5:19, 20).

Instead of live and let live, Paul calls Christians to responsible action. "If someone is caught in a sin, you who are spiritual should restore him gently" (Galatians 6:1). This presupposes the exercise of caring discernment.

What, then, did Jesus mean when He told His followers, "Do not judge, or you too will be judged"? First, consider a few of the words He used. The term *judge* literally meant to separate or choose. Consequently, it referred to determining guilt or truth, and then pronouncing judgment. The word was used both in a technical legal sense and in a more common, everyday sense.

The New Testament speaks of judging in both a positive and a negative manner. Romans 2:1-4 condemns those who judge others while failing to live up to their own professed standards. James insists that those who judge a brother actually sit in judgment of God's law (James 4:11). On the other hand, Jesus called for the crowds who followed Him to "stop judging by mere appearances, and make a right judgment" (John 7:24). On another occasion, He told them to "judge for yourselves what is right" (Luke 12:57).

Jesus painted a ridiculous picture when He portrayed one with a plank protruding from his eye attempting to help another remove a speck of sawdust from his eye. The terms were just as graphic in Jesus' language as they are in ours. The "plank" was a beam or wooden rafter used in first-century housing construction. The "speck" was just that, a tiny bit of sawdust or chaff.

What's the reality behind the exaggeration?

If you look closely, you'll see it isn't actually "judging" that Jesus condemned at all. He did not tell His followers to have nothing to do with sawdust-afflicted eyes. Quite to the contrary, He told them, "First take the plank out of your own eye, and *then* you will see clearly to remove the speck from your brother's eye" (Matthew 7:5). The solution is self-judging and compassionate sincerity.

The problems to which Jesus words apply are still very much a part of religious life. The two most common forms in which they appear are religious meanness and spiritual blindness.

Evil in God's Name. Religious meanness has always been one of Satan's most effective tools to dishonor the faith. Many unbelievers are well aware that much of history's most horrible events have been committed in the name of religion. The Crusades, the Protestant and Catholic wars in Ireland, the bloody battles between Muslims, Jews, and Christians in the Middle East, and countless other atrocities have been fired by faith. On a smaller scale, many a local congregation has been devastated by mean-tempered brothers and sisters.

In practical terms, what I have labeled "religious meanness" takes a variety of forms. In some, it's a fault-finding spirit. For some reason, many live as if their sole purpose in life were to locate problems in other believers' lives. If the spiritual detective work were for the purpose of helping, it might be understandable. More often, however, the fault-finding exists for one purpose—to find fault. In some, it's more than an occasional concern. It's a habitual preoccupation. It's this spirit that Jesus put off-limits for His followers.

In others, religious meanness takes the form of prejudice. Here lies the essential difference between the judgment Jesus condemned in Matthew 7:1, 2 and the discernment He condoned in Matthew 7:16. Prejudice makes judgments that go beyond the evidence or generalizes beyond the matter at hand. Such negative judging calls for second guessing a person's motives. It is one thing (a good and necessary thing) to regard as evil the actions of someone's life that breaches God's standards. It is an altogether different matter to infer the motive, intentions, or character of the person. Only God reads hearts (1 Samuel 16:7).

This was precisely what Paul had in mind when he wrote: "Who are you to judge someone else's servant? To his own master he stands or falls. . . . Why do you judge your brother? Or why do you look down on your brother? For we will all stand before God's judgment seat" (Romans 14:4, 10).

A third form of religious meanness is spiritual sadism. This attitude takes delight in seeing others suffer. A saintly believer once observed two preachers each deliver a sermon on Hell. When asked to compare the two messages, he noted that the first preacher announced that all the sinners present were going to Hell. The second preached the same truth. The difference, however, was that the first seemed glad about it, while the second spoke with tears in his eyes.

Many Pharisees were apparently afflicted with this malady. Jesus described their hateful inconsistency. "They tie up heavy loads and put them on men's shoulders," Jesus warned, "but they themselves are not willing to lift a finger to move them. . . . You shut the kingdom of heaven in men's faces. You yourselves do not enter, nor will you let those enter who are trying to" (Matthew 23:4, 13).

Some people mistakenly think they are closer to God when they are walking on top of others. They are wrong!

Spiritual Blindness. The other side of the inconsistency against which Jesus warned is spiritual blindness. Those affected can clearly see the slightest moral or spiritual problem in the life of another, but are totally oblivious to their own sin. Perhaps it is possible they are so preoccupied with inspecting others that they ignore themselves.

I read recently of a general who was reviewing a platoon of recruits who had just completed basic training. As he slowly walked past the line of soldiers, the officer searched for any sign of improper dress. Finally, he stopped in front of the last soldier and glared at him for several seconds.

Then he shouted in the private's face, "Soldier, fasten that button!"

The soldier, caught by surprise, hesitated, "Right now, sir?"

"Yes, right now! Fasten the button!"

The private then slowly reached up and began to fasten a loose button on the *general's* uniform!

Here lies the danger of judging. Often mote-seeking and beam-blindness go hand-in-hand. A spiritual advisor who is blind to his own weakness is a poor helper. As Paul warned those who seek to help another who is caught in sin,

> Watch yourself, or you also may be tempted. . . . If anyone thinks he is something when he is nothing, he deceives himself. Each one should test his own actions. Then he can take pride in himself, without comparing himself to somebody else, for each one should carry his own load (Galatians 6:1-5).

Insensitivity: Treating Everything Alike (Matthew 7:6)

Matthew 7:6 is one of the most difficult verses to understand in the entire Sermon on the Mount. It seems out of step with the tone of everything else Jesus has said, especially the preceeding section about judging. For centuries, scholars have wrestled with these words and produced countless conflicting interpretations.

The writer of the *Didache,* a Christian document from the early second century, applied the admonition to the Lord's Supper. "Let no man eat or drink of your Eucharist," he counseled, "except those baptized in the name of the Lord; for, as regards this, the Lord has said, 'Give not that which is holy unto dogs.'

Whether Jesus had such an application in mind is problematic at best!

The terms *dogs* and *pigs* were both expressions of contempt in Jewish society. The word for dog described the wild mongrels that scavenged the garbage of the city. Swine, of course, were the epitomy of uncleanness. Jesus would later speak of the kingdom in terms of a "pearl of great value" (Matthew 13:45, 46). Here he links the pearls with that which is "sacred."

In the context, these words provide a counterbalance to the preceeding admonition. While on the one hand, the disciple must avoid a judgmental, hyper-critical attitude, on the other hand, he must also not fall into a trap of indiscriminate activity. He must preserve a sense of spiritual sensitivity. Differences do exist in the world.

Disciples are vulnerable to two forms of insensitivity. First, we can grow calloused to the things of God. We begin to treat the kingdom matters as if they were no more than hog fodder. All things are not equal. If familiarity breeds contempt, it is altogether possible for those who are closest to the things of God to lose the sense of awe or specialness that once filled their hearts when they were new to the faith.

Second, disciples can grow insensitive to the differences in people. This has special application for those who would seek to share their faith with unbelievers or to help an erring brother. The temptation is to treat people as targets. In our zeal to share the faith (pass out the pearls), we can get so caught up in the activity that we forget the purpose.

Jesus' picture suggests three principles that every evangelist and people-helper needs to remember:

1. Not everyone wants help. Some with mote-infested eyes do not want the specks removed. Not all lost people want to hear the gospel. As sad as these facts may be to the believers, they are true.

2. We cannot force the gospel or our well-intentioned help on anyone. This doesn't mean that disciples should adopt a passive approach to evangelism—not at all! We simply must be wise enough to realize that the things of God cannot be forced on anyone. Evangelism dare not be reduced to spiritual mugging, where we attempt to jump some unsuspecting unbeliever and twist his arm until he confesses Christ.

Jesus wanted Jerusalem saved, but He consented to acknowledge the city's unbelief (Matthew 23:37). Paul desired that his fellow Jews accept Christ, but he also knew that there was a point beyond which his efforts were futile (Acts 13:44-51; 18:5, 6).

3. Third, the disciple must use appropriate common sense and discernment. He must exercise priorities and strategies in sharing the good news with the lost. He must learn the needs of those he wants to influence. He must earn the right to speak of sacred things to them. This is not an excuse for keeping the gospel to ourselves. Rather it is a call to make the most of our efforts.

Independence: Going It on Our Own (Matthew 7:7-11)

Another obstacle confronted by the disciple who becomes serious about his faith is an independent spirit. We can become proud of our accomplishments. Our attention focuses on what we have done or how far we have come. We develop a Godless religion that operates independently of the Lord.

The Pharisee, who paraded his religion for others to see without any regard for God, proves how possible such independence is (Matthew 6:1-18). Such an attitude goes hand-in-hand with pride (Luke 18:9-14).

What's the solution to an independent heart? Genuine, child-like prayer! A sense of total dependence on God!

It is a sad commentary on human nature that disciples need to be told to pray. One might think that praying would be second nature for those who follow Jesus. But it isn't. Prayer is hard work! Most of us find it much easier to do nearly anything else except pray.

On His last night, Jesus asked but one request of his men. "Watch and pray" (Matthew 26:36-46). But it was the one thing that was the hardest. They would have climbed mountains, weathered storms, or fought off the enemy for Him. But He just asked them to pray. And they failed.

His disciples must have sensed how hard prayer truly is. One of the few requests they made of Him was to teach them to pray! They never asked to learn how to walk on water, calm the storm, or even do mighty miracles. Prayer was the real issue, and they knew it.

Jesus knew that no disciple could begin the long trek down the straight and narrow unless he learned the lessons of prayer. He described prayer in two ways that on the surface appear contradictory.

First, prayer requires effort. It calls for persistent asking, seeking, knocking. It begins with a recognized need. One who is too proud to ask for help cannot pray. But prayer also calls for the effort that goes beyond simple asking. It requires seeking. This effort, in turn, demands persistence. A casual appeal for help and a half-hearted look for assistance will never suffice. A disciple who knows that he cannot go it alone will knock at the gates of God until he finds his source of supply.

Second, prayer requires childlike innocence and faith. The key to prayer is the willingness of God, not our persistence. We pray, even persistently, not because we think that our efforts will somehow force God to do things our way. Heaven forbid! We pray because we know our Father cares and has promised to help us. We pray confidently like a child who knows his father loves him, not presumptuously like a beggar demanding to be cared for.

Incompleteness: Losing the Love (Matthew 7:12)

With this verse, Jesus brought His call to moral excellence to its summit. This provides the keystone that holds all of the rest together. Many disciples, however, are surprised to learn that the principle Jesus announced was not altogether new.

"Love your neighbor" was a call as old as Scripture itself. The Old Testament is filled with the principle. The Jews were told to "love your neighbor as yourself" (Leviticus 19:18). This love did not stop with friends and fellow Jews, as many mistakenly think. The Old Testament taught the faithful to help an enemy in practical ways (Exodus 23:4, 5), to refuse to gloat over his misfortune (Proverbs 24:17), and even to feed him when he was hungry (Proverbs 25:21).

Even outside the Scriptures, one can find what appears to be examples of the Golden Rule. Epictitus, the Greek philosopher, told his disciples, "What you avoid suffering; seek not to inflict on others." Socrates said, "What stirs your anger when done by others, that do not to others." Aristotle, Confucious, and the learned rabbis of Jesus' day all told their followers not to do to others what they did not want done to them.

All of these statements sound like what Jesus taught. But the similarity is deceiving. A very basic difference exists. Each of these other examples was negative. They warned of harming a neighbor. Jesus called for a positive alternative. "Do to others what you would have them do to you" (Matthew 7:12).

This is the final danger of serious religion. A disciple can become so preoccupied with not making a mistake or harming another that he fails to recognize that Jesus asked for something more. The disciples' life must not be measured, Jesus suggests, by what evil he doesn't do, but by the good he does. A negative religion is always incomplete when compared to Jesus' standard.

The parable of the Good Samaritan provides a case in point (Luke 10:25-37). By the prevailing standards of the day, the priest and Levite did nothing wrong. They did not rob or beat the man in the ditch. Their consciences were clear. Not so, said Jesus. They didn't harm, but neither did they help, him. Consequently, they didn't love him!

At first glance, these four admonitions appear disconnected and isolated. But upon a closer inspection, we see that they stand together. Jesus refused to let His followers begin their walk of faith without knowing what was ahead. Because He wants born-again disciples, not just baptized Pharisees, Jesus posted signs beside the bumps on the straight and narrow.

Chapter Thirteen

Caution: Narrow Road Ahead
Matthew 7:13-27

For many, Jesus' conclusion to the Sermon on the Mount comes as a surprise. Most who think of this famous treatise recall the beauty of the Beatitudes, the stirring words on prayer and charity, or the unforgettable Golden Rule. While much of the sermon emphasizes love, peace, and forgiveness, the conclusion submits every reader and hearer to judgment.

Jesus left no doubt that what we have in the Sermon on the Mount is more than a collection of pleasing platitudes or sweet proverbs about being a happy person. More is at stake than that. The central theme throughout has been the kingdom—the rule of God. Jesus makes it clear that the kingdom is not a matter to be trifled with. It is a matter of ultimate importance.

The Real Jesus

This strong ending to the Sermon on the Mount provides a much needed corrective to the muddled thinking that surrounds Jesus today. Some mistakenly view Him as a good teacher and nothing more. They see Him as a moral cheerleader who went around affirming the good in people and calling them to be better. Much of the Sermon on the Mount fits this mold.

Others view Jesus pluralistically, as just one of many moral and religious options that are available in life, each with its assets and liabilities. Some choose Jesus. Others decide to follow Buddah, or Mohammed, or Marx. One is as valid as the others. It is simply a matter of choosing what's best for you at the moment.

This is how one young woman I recently baptized said her parents viewed her new religious zeal. "They think it's nice," she reported. "But they think it's just a phase. They think I'm a Christian right now like my younger sister was a vegetarian. 'She'll get over it eventually,' they say."

Even those of us who claim to be disciples of Jesus can slip into a less-than-honest view of Jesus if we're not careful. We can begin to think that Jesus' whole message was about how we could become happier, more fulfilled people rather than about the radical claims of the kingdom of God on our lives. Many believers have adopted what historian Martin Marty calls a "pick-and-choose Christianity." They view the demands of Jesus as a giant smorgasbord from which they can choose the parts they want to obey and leave the tougher items for someone else.

Jesus' conclusion to the Sermon on the Mount leaves little room for such distorted thinking. His teachings were given to be obeyed, He insisted, and anything less will meet with the severest judgment. At the heart of the warnings implicit in these final words is an understanding of who He is. Jesus clearly saw himself as more than a mild-mannered teacher. These words were not something that could be followed or ignored depending on the whim of the moment. Obedience or judgment were the only options.

The Unmovable Standard

The captain of a large naval ship watched a set of flashing lights slowly approaching in the dark fog. As the lights drew closer and closer, he ordered his signal man to flash a warning. "Alter your course ten degrees south."

Almost instantly a reply was received, "Alter your course ten degrees north."

The captain took little delight in his commands' being ignored. He ordered a second message, "Alter your course ten degrees south. I am Captain Brown."

Again the reply came back without the slightest delay. "Alter your course ten degrees north. I am Seaman Third Class Jones."

Immediately Captain Brown sent a third message. "Alter your course. This is a battleship!"

The third reply came back, "Alter your course. This is a lighthouse!"

Before we quarrel with Jesus' orders or grumble about the demands that He has placed on us, we need to remember with whom we are dealing. The King of kings takes orders from no one. His standard is unmovable. We can choose to ignore His directions, but the consequences will always be disastrous. This is the standard of the one who will judge the living and the dead.

Everything Jesus said in the Sermon on the Mount funnels down to this conclusion. In this final section, He offered three contrasts, the alternatives that face everyone who hears His words. For some, these are words of blessings and comfort. For others, they are just the opposite.

The Two Ways: Life and Death (Matthew 7:13, 14)

Jesus' first contrast resembles Moses' conclusion to ancient Israel's kingdom constitution. The old leader called his people to unswerving obedience.

> See, I set before you today life and prosperity, death and destruction. For I command you today to love the Lord your God, to walk in his ways, and to keep his commands, decrees and laws; then you will live and increase, and the Lord your God will bless you in the land you are entering to possess.
>
> But if your heart turns away and you are not obedient, and if you are drawn away to bow down to other gods and worship them, I declare to you this day that you will certainly be destroyed. You will not live long in the land you are crossing the Jordan to enter and possess.
>
> This day I call heaven and earth as witnesses against you that I have set before you life and death, blessings and curses. Now choose life, so that you and your children may live (Deuteronomy 30:15-29).

Jesus described two choices that confront humanity. He pictured two separate gates or entrances. One was wide and spacious. The other was narrow. The term for *narrow* came from a word meaning to groan. This gate was entered only with great difficulty and effort.

The two gates opened to two ways or paths. One was broad. The road found at the other side of the narrow gate was just as confining as its entrance. The two ways accommodated two different crowds. Many would enter through the wide gate and the broad way. Only a few would find the other, narrower path. But most significantly, one entrance led to life and the other to destruction. No clearer picture could be provided of two absolutely different choices and destinies.

Robert Frost's masterful poem *The Road Less Traveled* captures the spirit of the issue Jesus placed before His would-be disciples:

Two roads diverged in a yellow wood
And sorry I could not travel both
And be one traveler, long I stood
And looked down one as far as I could
To where it bent in the undergrowth. . . .

And both that morning equally lay
In leaves no steps had trodden black.
Oh, I kept the first for another day!
Yet, knowing how way leads on to way
I doubted if I should ever come back.

I shall be telling this with a sigh
Somewhere ages and ages hence:
Two roads diverged in a wood, and I—
I took the one less traveled by,
And that has made all the difference.

Jesus insisted that it does make a difference which path one takes in life. All roads do not lead to the same place. One leads to life and the other to death. And equally important, Jesus pictured only two ways—His and the way to death. He offered no medium road, one that is less evil, but not nearly so difficult. For Jesus— and for those who choose to follow Him—it is either/or!

What is it that Jesus taught with His picture of the narrow way? Simply this: there is something basically limiting about the path of discipleship. It can't be any other way. If discipleship means coming under the rule of God, then anything that compromises that must be done away with. He allows no other rival. Either He is Lord or He isn't. Either we love God with all our heart, soul, mind, and strength, or we don't.

The rich young ruler (Luke 18:18-30) learned this lesson with regrettable finality. When told to choose between his wealth and discipleship, he chose riches. Even though he regretted what he was doing, he wasn't prepared to walk the narrow way. Jesus' observation says it all, "Indeed, it is easier for a camel to go through the eye of a needle than for a rich man to enter the kingdom of God" (Luke 18:25).

Historians write of one of the ancient Christian shrines that became the site of frequent pilgrimages after the Crusades. The entrance to the shrine stood so low to the ground that a man could enter it only on his knees. They called it "Humility's Gate." The narrow gate of discipleship is like that. Anyone can walk the way, but only after he goes to his knees in submission to the rule of God. Admission is free, but many still find the price too high.

This is where grace and repentance come together. The way to Heaven is not for sale. No one can earn, buy, or work his way in. The door is always open, but some things must be left outside.

A legend of the fourteenth-century European Duke Raynald III illustrates an all too frequent fact of human nature. Raynald was a fat, intemperate person. His flawed character affected everything he did, including the way he ruled. After a violent quarrel, Raynald's brother Edward captained a revolt that overthrew him. Edward took Raynald prisoner but did not kill him.

Instead, he placed him in a specially constructed room in his castle. Edward told Raynald that he was free to leave the room and could even return to his throne once he left. The room however created a problem for the oversized Raynald. Each door and window to the room was left open but was constructed just small enough that Raynald could not pass through without first loosing the extra pounds that he needed to loose anyway.

Edward knew his brother's weakness. Each day, instead of posting a guard at the room, he would send quantities of delicious foods to his brother. Instead of shedding the pounds and walking out of the prison, Raynald grew fatter and fatter.

Accused of cruelty, Edward simply replied, "My brother is not a prisoner. He may leave whenever he wills."

Ten years later, when Edward was killed in a battle, Raynald was finally released. By that time, his health was so ruined that he died within a year.

This is Jesus' picture of the narrow gate and the eye of the needle. The way is open to all. Yet is is so narrow that few find it. It is both free and costly. Discipleship is a way of grace. But only those willing to submit to the rule of God can enter it.

The Two Trees: True and False (Matthew 7:15-23)

Jesus' next contrast assumed three basic facts of religious life. First, He assumed that true and false, right and wrong do exist. All beliefs or convictions are not equal. Some claims are valid; others are not. Second, some teachers and prophets are true and others are false. Finally, the difference between the true and the false is recognizable. These facts presuppose a standard against which all religious claims are measured.

Jesus used two different metaphors to portray the nature of false prophets. First, like a wolf in sheep's clothing, they are *deceptive*. What they are really like cannot be determined by a superficial examination. If the counterfeit were easily distinguished from the genuine article, it would pose only a minor difficulty. But its very purpose is to deceive and confuse. Paul used similar language to describe the false teachers he battled.

> For such men are false apostles, deceitful workman, masquerading as apostles of Christ. And no wonder, for Satan himself masquerades as an angel of light. It is not surprising, then, if his servants masquerade as servants of righteousness (2 Corinthians 11:13-15).

Jesus further insisted that the *difference* between the true and false prophets is found in the fruit. Their character and the results of their efforts give them away. A wolf may masquerade as a sheep, but eventually, when it grows hungry enough, its wolf-nature will come to light. A tree may also look like something it is not. Whatever the similarities in appearance, the harvest will reveal the truth. Only the genuine article bears genuine fruit.

Perhaps a Christmas tree provides a better example for us. I can bring a tree into my house, trim it, decorate it, and even make it look like a live tree. But no matter how hard I try, eventually the needles will turn brown and begin to fall to the carpet. I can hang plastic apples on the tree. They may look fresh and tasty, but as soon as I try to eat one of the plastic variety, I will soon be reminded of the truth. I can even fasten real apples to my Christmas tree as part of the decorations, but that won't make the tree an apple tree. Eventually, the fruit on my counterfeit tree will rot. The dying tree can never be anything other than what it is. No amount of decorations can change it into a fruit tree.

Telling a sheep apart from a wolf or one kind of tree from another may be one thing, but prophets and teachers are another matter. How do you tell them apart? Jesus says it is by their fruit. However, this can be a bit misleading. For some, fruit might mean success, wealth, or any of a variety of human criteria. For Jesus, fruit meant something much more specific.

Rather than spell out how His disciples are to distinguish the false from the true prophets, Jesus told how He will do it at the final judgment. Two things will not matter then: profession and performance. Some will claim that they knew who Jesus was and that they had performed mighty deeds in His name, but to no avail. Only one thing will matter—whether or not they obeyed the will of the Father.

We come again to the same truth we have seen over and over again. Jesus came to introduce men and women to the kingdom of God. This kingdom is the personal rule of God in the lives of people who voluntarily submit to His authority. It is a matter of the heart. Ritual, rules, and religious activities may all have their place, but none are a substitute for the rule of God. A false prophet may on occasion say the right words. He may openly submit to the rituals, but his heart will remain far from God.

Whether the false prophets Jesus pictured at the judgment had actually done all they claimed or not is an open question. One thing is clear: their alleged miracles were beside the point. He sought something other than miraculous works; He wanted a changed heart.

Unfortunately, many well-intentioned people in our day are not sure what to make of Jesus' words. Having abandoned any solid standard against which to measure truth and error, they have no idea what to do with the concept of "false prophets." The words seem old-fashioned. Jesus knew what the words *false prophet* meant. Those who desire to be His disciples, now even as then, ought to learn from Him.

For most of us reading these pages, however, there is a more pressing problem. Most of us have a fairly clear idea of right and wrong, truth and error. Some of us are certain we know exactly who the false prophets of our day are. Not only that, we are more than happy to point them out.

Our problem is the temptation to major in minors. We easily slip into a negative, defensive posture that keeps us so busy fighting false prophets that we never find time to preach the gospel. We are so zealous about exposing the false to the brothers that we fail to proclaim the truth to the lost.

We need to be reminded that the best antidote to heresy is not inexhaustible knowledge of every potential error, but a personal knowledge of the truth. Those who are trained to detect counterfeit currency do not simply learn the tricks of the forgers. They study the genuine article so thoroughly that the false stands out in contrast.

Haddon Robinson tells the story of a young Chinese boy who wanted to learn about jade. His mentor placed a piece of jade in his hand and told him to hold it tight. While the boy held the stone, the teacher spoke with him of many subjects. But not once did he discuss the jade. Some time later, he took the jade from the boy and sent him home.

The next day the lad returned. The old man repeated the events of the previous day. He placed the stone in the boy's hand and talked quietly with him, but never about the jade.

The scene was repeated day after day. The boy grew frustrated that his teacher refused to speak to him of jade, but he was too polite to protest. Finally, one day, the boy arrived for his lesson and the old man placed the stone in his hand again.

This time the boy looked down with a startled expression on his face. By all appearances, the stone was just like the others he held each day. But he knew.

"This isn't jade," he protested.

The old man simply smiled and nodded.

The Two Builders: Hearing and Doing (Matthew 7:24-27)

The scene Jesus described in His story of the two builders could have been a familiar one in His day. Palestine is an arid region. Dry river beds criss-cross the countryside. Most of the year, these waddis are little more than flat, sandy stretches in the wilderness. But when the rainy season comes, they can become instant rivers with torrents of raging water rushing down to the distant river valleys. Sometimes, a particular river bed might go years without there ever being enough rain to flood it.

Why would anyone build a house on such a spot? Perhaps ignorance. A new resident unfamiliar with the terrain of a particular area might think that flat low-lying piece of property was an ideal place for a house. More than likely, however, the unfortunate builder knew what he was doing. He just thought he would be an exception. Building on the sandy bottom land was easier, much quicker, and probably less expensive than carting the materials to the top of a hill and then trying to fasten the foundation into solid rock.

He probably knew the dangers of flash floods, but they happened so seldom that the odds of his house getting hit were fairly remote!

A few blocks from where I live, a small river winds across the prairie and through our small city. A few years ago, a unusually heavy summer rain forced the normally quiet river out of its banks and into the streets, basements, and even living rooms of many families.

They all knew that such a flood was possible. When they bought their homes, they were required to buy federal flood insurance. The Army Corps of Engineers had even done calculations on the flood potential of the area. Most folks felt secure in the knowledge that the Corps said that a flood large enough to reach the homes was likely to happen only once every fifty years.

Most people bought their homes or built new ones knowing the danger, but never really expecting to see it become reality.

Unlike the homes in this midwestern flood plain, the house of the foolish builder wasn't able to withstand the rampaging waters. The rains came. The riverbed didn't just slowly fill with water. Suddenly, out of nowhere, a sudden rush of water and mud came tumbling down the valley washing away the rocks, shrubs, and *houses* in its path. It was a total disaster.

Both the wise and foolish man built houses. As far as we know, each took equal care in building. Other than in location, both houses were apparently well built and cared for. Also, both houses encountered storms. The one difference between the two houses was the most important.

Obviously, Jesus wasn't just telling a cute story about two contractors. As He explained, He was talking about people and how they respond to His teaching. Many people hear His words. But according to Jesus, some are wise and some are foolish. The difference is not a matter of intelligence, personal aptitude, or even opportunity. The difference is much more basic. Some hear His teachings. Others hear and obey.

For true discipleship, *doing,* not just knowing or hearing is the issue. James taught the same truth when he wrote:

> Do not merely listen to the word, and so deceive yourselves. Do what it says. Anyone who listens to the word but does not do what it says is like a man who looks at his face in a mirror and, after looking at himself, goes away and immediately forgets what he looks like. But the man who looks intently into the perfect law that gives freedom, and continues to do this, not forgetting what he has heard, but doing it—he will be blessed in what he does" (James 1:22-25).

"Obey everything I have commanded" has always been the challenge of Jesus (Matthew 28:20). That was what He expected of His apostles. It is also what He expects of His twentieth-century followers. Disobedience is the contradiction of faith. It is to refuse the rule of God.

Peter Marshall, the late chaplain of the U. S. Senate, was once asked to present a method of Bible study to a gathering of prominent citizens. Reportedly, Marshall advised his listeners to begin their Bible reading with Matthew 5.

> Begin with Matthew 5:1. Continue reading until you find a scripture telling you to do something you are not doing or telling you to stop doing something you are presently doing. When you come to that point, stop reading. Mark your place and then go and do what the Bible has told you to do. Once you have mastered that lesson, then and only then, return to your Bible and begin reading where you stopped. Once again read until you find some instruction that you need to personally apply. Stop at that point and go do what you should before returning to the Scriptures.

"I guarantee you," said Marshall, "that if you read the Bible this way, you will not only change your life, you will change the world before you finish Matthew 7!"

Whether or not this procedure makes for good Bible study or not, it certainly catches the intent Jesus had for His teachings. Dietrich Bonhoffer summarized this well in his classic *The Cost of Discipleship* (pp. 218, 219):

> Humanly speaking we could understand and interpret the Sermon on the Mount in a thousand different ways. Jesus knows only one possibility: simple surrender and obedience, not interpreting it and applying it, but doing and obeying it. That is the only way to hear His word. But again he does not mean that it is to be discussed as an ideal, he really means us to get on with it."

The Easier Way

Jesus never promised that the way of discipleship would be easy. In fact, He warned that it could be quite costly. But He also promised that this way, as straight and narrow as it may be, leads to life. In the long run, the way of discipleship—seeking first His kingdom—proves to be the easier way. As difficult as it may sometimes be to follow Jesus, it is always harder to walk alone.

That's why He promised, "Surely, I am with you always."